The Girl Who Doesn't Talk

The Girl Who Doesn't Talk

Beyond Shy: A Journey Through
Severe Social Anxiety Disorder

SUSANNA KLEIN

iUNIVERSE, INC.
BLOOMINGTON

The Girl Who Doesn't Talk
Beyond Shy: A Journey through Severe Social Anxiety Disorder

iUniverse books may be ordered through booksellers or by contacting:

iUniverse
1663 Liberty Drive
Bloomington, IN 47403
www.iuniverse.com
1-800-Authors (1-800-288-4677)

ISBN: 978-1-4759-6466-0 (sc)
ISBN: 978-1-4759-6468-4 (hc)
ISBN: 978-1-4759-6467-7 (e)

Library of Congress Control Number: 2012922558

Printed in the United States of America

iUniverse rev. date: 12/13/2012

Contents

PART 2

Prologue: A Turning Point

I first uttered a word in school in the third grade. It was the first day of school. We were all sitting at our desks, with Mrs. Foster at the front of the room. Mrs. Foster was older. She would retire in the middle of my third-grade year. She was also of German descent and had a strong accent. She was known for being very strict. Everyone feared her.

One of the kids said to me, "Mrs. Foster is mean. She'll make you talk."

I was sitting toward the front of the class, with my hands folded on my desk like we all had to do, while Mrs. Foster took roll. As she said everyone's name, we were supposed to say, "Yes, Ma'am." My last name started with "O," so I had to wait a while until I heard my name. I was nervous the whole time. When it was my turn, she looked right at me and said, "Susanna."

Silence.

After a few minutes one of the kids said, "She's here. She doesn't talk."

"I asked Susanna," said Mrs. Foster. "Susanna, say 'Yes, Ma'am.'"

Another silence, this time longer. I don't know how many minutes went by, but they were full of decision-making for me—and shame. I was afraid to talk, and I was afraid of Mrs. Foster. Finally, she won, and so did I.

"Yes, Ma'am," I said in a small voice.

"Praise the Lord!" said Mrs. Foster.

A couple of kids whispered, "She talked!"

Part 1

Chapter 1: A Sensitive Child

I don't know what I would have done without my siblings. They were my friends and playmates. We have always been a close family. Not perfect of course, but still my lifeline.

The only place where I was completely at ease as a child was at home with my parents, my brother, my two sisters, and my grandmother.

From the time I was three years old until I turned twelve, we lived in a tiny house in a neighborhood on the poor side of Greenville, Missouri. We had shag carpets over the hardwood floors, and an olive green kitchen that my mother immediately painted yellow. We had four bedrooms, which we put to good use.

The bedroom I shared with my sister was dark and cozy, with dark paneling on the walls. We often played there in the afternoon, and it often smelled like my grandmother's cooking during those times. The only thing she made that I hated was stuffed green peppers. I was so disappointed every time she made those. But overall she was a good cook. I especially liked her meringues.

My handsome, dark-haired little brother, Rafael, was always taking things apart to see how they worked. When his curiosity led him to dismantle something, sometimes he didn't know how to put it back together.

As a teenager, Rafael had some friends who were into computers. They usually came over late at night, went into Rafael's room to use the computer, and did not come out until dawn. Rafael's computer skills learned in the secret of night got him his first real job.

Rafael was known as a man of few words, but when he spoke, it was always good. Every deadpan thing he said was either hilarious or profoundly smart.

Rafael has never been a water person, but when he was little he was afraid of the water and hated it. At swimming lessons he would cling to his instructor's neck the whole time. He was into tae-kwon-do for a while, and liked to practice his kicks on us, coming within inches of our face. "Stop it!" I would yell. I think it was fun for him to see my reaction.

My sister Monica was a classic middle child. She used to get sad when our dad would say, "Susanna is special because she's the oldest. Rafael is special because he's the only boy. Isabel is special because she's the youngest. And Monica is special because...she's Monica!"

Monica, with her sexy good looks, long black hair, and dark skin, always had friends surrounding her and boys looking at her. It seemed important to her to fit in with her peers. When she grew up and finally found herself, she turned out to be full of artistic talent.

My youngest sister Isabel was my parents' surprise. Her fair skin and lighter brown hair made her look different from the rest of us. People used to ask our mom where Isabel had come from, or whether she was adopted. Mom hated that. In public, we used to send Isabel to ask for things for us, or to talk to people, when we were too embarrassed. She was the only one of us who would dare. When we went to the photographer to have our picture taken, Isabel wore her smile all the way there. She enjoyed talking to people and being the center of attention.

My siblings and I used to play together for hours. One time we spent a wonderful weekend at Tan-Tar-A resort, so we played "Tan-Tar-A" at home a lot after that. We made a car out of the sofa cushions. Sitting behind our sofa cushion "dashboard," we "drove" to Tan-Tar-A to enjoy our resort.

One of my favorite things to play was Little People. We would set up game boards into two- or three-level houses, using blocks to raise the game boards. We added little furniture and people. Or sometimes it was a one-level building made of blocks, with different rooms. I liked to draw refrigerators, sinks, dressers, and windows on the blocks. We made stores, schools, or churches. Then we acted out the story we were imagining. Often we got so excited about our fun that we had to poop. We knew it was a good game if it made us have to poop.

We also loved playing "beauty pageant." After watching a pageant on TV, during which we made fun of all the contestants, we would parade around the living room in our best clothes, then line up to see who had won "Miss America." Sometimes we fought over who got to be the winner.

One time we were all playing in the backyard, when one of us found a red object buried in the dirt. I was afraid of that thing because I thought it could be the devil. I had seen that picture of the red devil with the forked tail on those cans of chicken. For quite a while my siblings and I debated whether we should dig up the red thing. Finally we took the plunge and dug deeper, and found that it was just a piece of plastic. No devil in the backyard.

I was a very sensitive child. When I turned three years old my grandmother made me a doll piñata. It was beautiful, with a full pink dress, black hair, and white skin. I loved it. Then my dad took it outside and hung it on a rope. All the kids started beating my doll with a stick. I began screaming and crying, running inside to hide. My grandmother understood, and asked my mother to stop the piñata hitting. She did, and I got my piñata doll back, not too damaged. What a relief.

At my preschool, we always walked to Smith Park, all holding onto a rope so nobody would get lost. Everyone wanted a turn being first, and the second most coveted position was last. So we took turns. One day I wasn't paying attention and just randomly picked up the end of the rope, instead of holding on to the middle. The kid whose turn it was to be last snatched the rope from me and said, "It's MY turn to be last!" I was crushed.

Another time in preschool I participated in Show and Tell. Everyone sat in a circle, and we took turns walking around the inside of the circle, showing off our items. When it was my turn, I started out fine, showing my Humpty Dumpty on a string. I was pleased, but embarrassed, when the teacher said, "What in the world?" But then I felt too self-conscious to finish walking the circle, so I gave up and sat down.

At Thanksgiving time we drew turkeys by tracing the outline of our hands. Without thinking, I drew a mouth with teeth on my turkey. One of the other kids said, "Turkeys don't have teeth!" I realized he was right, and I was mortified.

During Vacation Bible School one summer, we were making a craft and my glue was not working very well. I said, "This doesn't stick," but nobody heard me. I'm sure I could have repeated myself more loudly and someone would have helped me, but I felt embarrassed and decided to stay quiet instead. I didn't realize at the time how important this incident was.

Chapter 2: So This Is Public School

For Kindergarten and the first half of first grade, I attended Weller, the neighborhood elementary school across the street from our house. Before I started school, we spoke Spanish at home. I understood English, because I heard it in public every day, but I did not use it. When I started school it was all in English. On my first day of Kindergarten, I decided that until I felt more comfortable with English, I wouldn't talk much. I never meant to insist on silence, but that is what happened. I told my mom that I would talk when Denver, our dog, talked. Soon I became "the girl who doesn't talk." Whenever we had a substitute teacher, or someone met me for the first time and did not understand my silence, the other children always came to my defense. "Susanna doesn't talk," they said. The longer I went without talking, the harder it was to break the habit. Even when I felt a little more comfortable, I could not bring myself to speak because, as I explained to my parents, "Everyone will get too excited."

One day in Kindergarten we were having recess indoors and I was playing with Lincoln Logs. I decided to make grass with the short pieces, standing them all on end to make my "lawn." I was having a really good time, thinking I was building something great, until another kid came by and said,

"You can't have that many people standing all together. That's a fire hazard!"

I really wanted to say, "These aren't people. This is grass!"

But I could not. The boy continued playing with the Lincoln Logs. I doubt he was trying to take them away from me. He probably just wanted to join in. But I was crushed. Embarrassed and frustrated at my inability to speak what was on my mind, I stopped playing with the Lincoln Logs and let the other kid have them.

Another time in Kindergarten, I could not get my scissors to work, but I was too afraid to ask for help. So I just struggled quietly for a long time. Fortunately, the teacher noticed that I was having trouble and when she looked closely, she saw that I was trying to use left-handed scissors. She gave me right-handed scissors instead, and then everything was fine.

Every recess I would go outside and stand under a tree—always the same tree, every recess, alone. I could not run and play with the other kids. I simply did not know how and I was too afraid. Eventually a couple of sixth-grade girls noticed me standing there. They began talking to me, and when I did not respond, they tried to convince me to talk to them. I fascinated them; Hispanic children were rare in Greenville in the 1970s. Those girls could not resist playing with my long, dark, curly hair. In the first few days of school, I had latched onto a little piece of paper in my coat pocket. It was a piece of trash, but it brought me comfort. I always had my hand in my coat pocket, playing with the little piece of paper. When the girls noticed that, one of them took my little paper. I was distressed, but finally, to my relief, a teacher told them to leave me alone.

By far the most embarrassing thing that happened to me at Weller School was the incident with the naked doll. We were having indoor recess and I was playing by myself with some Barbie dolls. I was pretending that they were taking a bath, just like I did at home. Of course when you take a bath you take your clothes off, so I took off Barbie's clothes and made her walk naked into the pretend bathroom for her tub bath. Some of the kids saw me walking this naked doll around, and they told the sixth-grade girls that were watching our class while our teacher was out that I was being nasty, showing off the naked doll to the boys. I was innocent, but I could not defend myself. Our babysitters made me sit at my desk and not play anymore that whole recess. I was crushed and mortified, almost in tears. But even that did not enable me to tell the girls that it had all been a mistake. When Mrs. Beaman, our regular teacher, got back, she immediately understood the situation. She said, "Susanna would never do that."

She asked me if I was OK. That must have helped some, but all I remember is the unfairness and humiliation that came from my inability to say something. No wonder I came home from school in a bad mood much of the time—I had so much frustration built up inside.

Then there was the incident of the cricket in my dress. During class one day I felt something at the back of my neck moving around. It was not a tag on the dress. It was weirder and more horrifying. But I could not figure out what it was and I could not bring myself to ask for help. So I suffered silently, until the boy behind me said, "Teacher, Susanna has a bug in her dress. I'll get it." He got it, and I was so relieved and grateful. That boy was my hero that day.

Around Christmas time I drew a manger scene in class. One of the other kids noticed what I was drawing, and asked me to draw one for him. I did, and pretty soon several kids wanted me to draw them pictures. I was annoyed and didn't want to draw for everyone, but I couldn't tell them "no."

I was really having trouble interacting with my classmates, so my parents arranged for me to have some play dates with a girl from my class who lived down the street. They thought it would help me relax at school. It was a good idea, but it didn't work. We did not really make friends. One time she did not want to be at our house at all, but her parents made her stay. I talked to her a little at our house, but never at school.

The best day I had at Weller School was my last one. I was sitting in music class, learning "DO, a deer, a female deer; RE, a drop of golden sun..." The principal briefly interrupted class to tell me that my parents were there to pick me up early. They told me that they were taking me out of that school, and I was going to a new one. I was surprised and so happy! What a relief! I wasn't sad or nostalgic at all. I was just so glad to get out of that scary place forever.

Chapter 3: Therapy

My parents sought professional help for me when I was in Kindergarten, first, and second grade. They first took me to a psychiatrist, who tested me. He said I was brilliant. He also recommended that my parents spend a lot of time with me. When he noticed how I crept up behind my daddy and clung to his neck, he said that physical touch was essential and that they needed to hold me closely. I'm pretty sure this was not a new idea to them. The psychiatrist also said that I needed time to work through the difficulties, and that the school was not offering the help they should have.

By the school's recommendation, Mom and Dad then took me to a child psychologist, who had several sessions with me but could not come up with anything useful. According to my parents, she did not seem to know what she was doing.

The only thing that helped, according to my dad's memories, was when he suggested recording my voice and playing it to the class. He said that seemed to make me more comfortable with others hearing my voice.

Dad also said that even though the teachers were not helpful, the other kids were. One little girl often said to people, "Susanna doesn't talk," or in other words, "leave her alone."

All I remember about my therapy is a big room with an easel for painting. I enjoyed going for therapy because I could play with all the toys, and best of all, I could paint. My parents say that the therapists told them I was being manipulative. They thought I enjoyed the attention I got from not talking. They were wrong.

Chapter 4: A New Start

After my parents pulled me out of Weller School, they put me in a private school, Christian Schools of Greenville. As soon as I walked into my new classroom, I felt better. It was smaller, cozier, and more comfortable than where I had come from. There was carpet on the floor, the room was smaller, and the teacher was younger and prettier, with her long straight hair. The desks were one piece, with the chair attached to the little table, and a space underneath for our books and supplies.

I arrived a little late my first day, but the teacher stopped what she was doing to introduce me to the class. Then she told everyone to take out their Big Chief pads. I was used to everyone making a big noise when it was time to get out supplies, so I banged to the floor, and immediately realized I was the only one thumping my bones to the floor with such fanfare. I felt very embarrassed, and finished getting my paper quietly like everyone else.

Even though nobody here knew me as the girl who didn't talk, and this school was much smaller than my last one, I still didn't talk. I really wanted to be normal and make friends, but I couldn't.

I don't remember very many of my first-grade classmates, but I do remember curly dark-haired Jessica, because she always called me Miss Priss, which hurt my feelings. I was glad the day she vomited in school and got sent home early.

One of my favorite things about first grade was playing 7-Up when we couldn't go outside to play. Everyone put their heads down on their desks, closed their eyes, and stuck out one thumb. Seven people were chosen to go around the room, touching people's thumbs. If their thumbs got touched, they had to put them down. Then everyone lifted their heads and tried to guess who had touched their thumbs. Once I fooled everyone because

I knew they all expected me to be gentle, so I touched thumbs roughly. Nobody ever guessed it was I.

In second grade, I used to misspell words on purpose on my spelling pretest, because those who spelled every word correctly got to go out for an extra recess. Those who missed words on the pretest had to take the test again. I did not like standing alone at recess. I preferred to stay inside and take the test again.

During recess one day, one of the girls I was with said, "She's so skinny. Maybe she's from a country where there's not enough to eat." She seemed kind and concerned, not like she was trying to make fun of me. But it hurt when kids talked about me as if I weren't there.

Every morning we had to stand and say the pledge to the American flag, the pledge to the Christian flag, and the pledge to the Bible. That presented a problem for me because I did not speak in school. I did not want to disobey or be disrespectful by not reciting the pledges, but I didn't want anyone to hear my voice or even see my lips move either. So I taught myself how to talk without moving my lips: "I tledge allegiance to the thlag oth the United States oth Anerica." I don't know if I successfully fooled anyone, but as far as I was concerned, I was the only one who knew I was saying the pledge.

Even though my third-grade teacher, Mrs. Foster, was an instrument of positive change for me, and good at heart, I did not like her. I did not do well with such a gruff personality. One time we were learning our division tables, and I had not felt like doing my homework. When it came time to turn it in, I did not have mine. The students who did not do their work got a spanking with a ruler on their hands. Even me. I could tell it made my teacher sad to have to spank me, but she had to be fair. I had to walk to her desk at the front of the class and receive my swat.

A girl in our class was a little quieter and more sensitive than most. One day the teacher called her to her desk up front. She did not want to go, because she was afraid to be spanked in front of everyone. She hesitated, tears beginning to form in her eyes. Finally, Mrs. Foster waited her out and made her come to the front, just like she had smoked me out of my silence. The little girl stood in front of Mrs. Foster's desk, expecting the worst, and Mrs. Foster surprised her by presenting her with a necklace, a reward for a job exceptionally done. The girl cheered up and took her gift proudly back to her desk.

That is the effect Mrs. Foster had on us, and she did not soften it for the shy and sensitive ones. She expected a lot from us, she enforced strict discipline, and most students ended up appreciating it. When Mrs. Foster left in the middle of the year, every student cried, except three: a boy, a tomboy, and me. I was glad she was leaving. Yes, I did need someone to push me to overcome my fears, but not with military pressure.

After Mrs. Foster left, we got a new teacher, Mrs. Nelson. Mrs. Nelson was much younger, and she looked strong and wore her hair very short. She was much less strict than Mrs. Foster, and I felt more comfortable around her. But that did not make it any easier for me to ask for help when I needed it.

Our class was learning long division, and I didn't understand very well. I was having trouble and getting very frustrated. But I was too shy to ask for help, so I suffered in silence. Then I couldn't hold it in any longer—I began to cry. Our new teacher noticed that I was crying softly, and she asked me what was wrong, but I could not tell her. So she called my parents, and my daddy came by to find out what was wrong and to comfort me. He brought me McDonald's for lunch and we ate it together in the car. After lunch, Mrs. Nelson helped me understand long division.

When I was in fourth grade, my brother was in second grade. I was happy to find out that they had combined second and fourth grade, and I would be in my brother's class. Then I learned that they had done it so I could be more comfortable, and I was embarrassed. However, I did enjoy having my brother in my class. They really went out of their way to help me. That was a good thing to do, but it still was not enough.

Fourth grade was one of my best years in school. My teacher was Miss Smith, a popular unmarried teacher, the one I had had for second grade. I was beginning to feel more comfortable using my voice in school, and actually enjoyed answering questions in class. We often played games like Around the World, where two students stood next to each other, and whoever answered a question correctly first got to continue to compete with the next student, and so on. I enjoyed being able to beat everyone, except a boy named Tony, in the math games.

One time we had some free time to draw with markers, a special thing to us. I loved art most of all in school, maybe because I could express myself without having to talk, and it was fun. So I was drawing a McDonald's meal, and an apple with a worm coming out of it. When another student saw it, she wanted me to draw her one, and as other kids saw my drawings, they each wanted me to draw them one too. That made me feel important.

The same kids who had been popular in first grade were still popular in fourth. In first grade I had secretly called them "The Bloodhound Gang," for some reason. I knew I could never belong, but I was OK with that because in fourth grade I had a best friend named Michelle.

Michelle was from Guam and had been adopted into a family with a lot of children—some foster, some adopted, and some biological. Sometimes I spent the night at her house. I liked being with Michelle, but I did not like spending the night at her house much. I was always hungry there. It wasn't like at my house where you could grab a snack anytime you wanted. And of course I wasn't going to ask for something to eat.

One morning we had pancakes for breakfast, but they had run out of syrup, so we had to eat them dry. The cats were allowed to walk on the table and eat scraps. And worst of all, they didn't have enough sleeping bags to go around, so one time I had to share a sleeping bag with my friend. It was a tight squeeze and I had a big personal bubble. But what could I do? I finally went to sleep, counting the hundreds of owls my friend's mom collected. I was relieved the next morning when my mom came to pick me up.

Chapter 5: Not So Well-Liked Anymore

After my fourth-grade year, my parents moved us to Pleasant View Elementary School. I did not like fifth or sixth grade. The public school was much bigger than the private Christian school, and I felt overwhelmed. I didn't know anybody. I was not mute anymore, thank God, but I was still profoundly shy. And it seemed I was no longer liked and protected. In those later grades I was teased and left out for being so withdrawn.

One day in fifth grade a girl said something that hurt my feelings. I don't remember what it was, but it made my whole body hurt. After school I went into my room and lay across my bed, numb and in pain at the same time. I suffered over her words.

Indoor recess consisted of me sitting alone at my desk. Every once in a while someone would invite me to play the board game *Trouble* with them, and I liked that. But I was never brave enough to initiate anything myself. I preferred it when the teacher led a class game like Twister. I didn't really have friends that year.

We did fractions in fifth grade. Math was hard for me, but during seatwork time I got brave enough to go up to our teacher's desk to ask for help. I did that repeatedly. But I did have to make myself do it, pushing back the nervous feelings and asking my questions anyway. That was an improvement from my early elementary years when I could only sit and cry.

In sixth grade, a bully named Trixie made my life miserable. She was always teasing me, like she did to anyone who wasn't part of the "in crowd." She pulled my braids all the time. When I said, "Stop," she mocked me in a whiny little voice. One time all her friends got mad at her for bothering me so much. They took my side. So then she got mad at me for "taking away all her friends." When she realized she had gone too far, she came out to me at recess (of course I was standing alone) to apologize. It was chilly out and her arms were crossed across her chest with goose bumps on them. I said it was OK, but it wasn't. She had hurt me and made me feel stupid.

Another time I was using the bathroom, and Trixie came in with some friends. She pushed my stall door open, knowing I was in there, looked at her friends, and pointed and laughed at me sitting there on the toilet. All I could do was stare back, humiliated.

Probably the worst part of school was organized play, usually softball. The teacher picked two team captains, who took turns picking their team members one at a time, until everyone had been chosen. The athletes and the popular kids would get picked first. Last were the tiny kids, the overweight ones, and the shy ones. Only the fat kids got picked after me, sometimes having to be assigned to a team by the teacher, because neither of the team captains wanted them on their team.

I was terrible at sports. I hated it when it was my turn to hit the ball and the pitcher moved closer so it would be easier for me to hit it. They were probably just being kind, but I wanted to be treated like everyone else. And Trixie was always there to make fun of the way I hit the ball or the way I ran and got tagged out.

I never broke the rules in school, which is why Trixie called me a "Goody Two-Shoes." One time I was writing with a pen that looked like a bottle of pink nail polish. The teacher, Mrs. Adler, a heavy-set woman with black hair and a serious, strict manner, scolded me for painting my nails in class. But she soon realized it was only a pen, and said it was OK and she was sorry. That's the closest I came to "getting in trouble."

In sixth grade the girls could finally try out for cheerleading. Every indoor recess that winter, everyone pushed the desks back against the walls. The boys practiced breakdancing. They thought they were cool with their perms in the back of their hair. The girls practiced their cheerleading routines. Michael Jackson was a popular heartthrob back then, so *Thriller* and *Beat It* were the songs of choice for their routines.

Only three girls in the class did not try out for cheerleading. I could not imagine cheerleading, and I did not feel bad about it. I don't remember what I did when everyone was practicing—probably look at my sticker books that were popular then, or read, or play a board game with a girl who tried to befriend me.

I was definitely different from my preteen peers, but all I wanted was to be normal, like everyone else. I really appreciated my sixth-grade Sunday school teachers because they treated me like everyone else, instead of tiptoeing around me and being extra nice.

Chapter 6: Spain

In 1984 we went to Spain on special missionary assignment for my dad's sabbatical, so he could teach in a Bible school. I went into a mild depression. At twelve and thirteen years old, I felt like I no longer enjoyed childhood things much, but I also wasn't ready for adult things yet.

I got sad and depressed when someone used the word "life," because it reminded me of the futility of life. I was trying to come up with some reason for life, some point to it, even though I knew about God and our purpose. I just did not feel it. I loved the word "enjoy," because I wanted to believe that enjoying something made it all worthwhile, and was a reason for life.

I liked seventh grade at Evangelical Christian Academy (ECA). Most of the students were missionary kids, and some were from military families. They treated me nicely, and I wasn't a reject.

One time the kids were rearranging the desks, and they decided to put the cool kids on one side of the room and the uncool ones on the other. I felt bad for the kids in the "uncool" group, but I was elated to discover that they considered me one of the cool kids. But part of me wondered if they just didn't want to hurt shy little Susanna's feelings.

By seventh grade I knew I couldn't be silent. I had to talk when spoken to. But my conversations went something like this:

"What's your name?"

"Susanna."

"Do you have plans for lunch?"

"I forgot to bring my lunch."

"Would you like to come to my house for lunch?"

"OK."

I didn't exactly hold up my end of the conversation, since every word was a struggle and I felt self-conscious. I could rarely bring myself to initiate conversations, not with very many people around. And I had not the skills or the calm presence of mind to keep a good conversation going. So at school I was very quiet.

For our speech class that year, I memorized a humorous speech and presented it in front of all the parents. It probably was not funny when I gave the speech and I was extremely nervous, but I did it! That was definitely a victory for me. People said I did well and mine was the most enjoyable. It was a small boost for my self-esteem.

My feelings got hurt easily. When I mistakenly had my long, curly, dark hair cut short in a style better suited for straight hair, I had to be brave to go to school the next day, knowing I looked totally different. People said, "I like your hair. It's cute," but I could tell they were just being polite. That suspicion was confirmed when I overhead a boy say to a girl, "Her hair *was* great." It took years to get over my dread of going to a beauty salon.

In seventh grade I first began noticing and liking boys. I had a crush on a twelfth-grade boy, a tall, dark and curly-haired Italian guy with a nice, fun personality. But I never told anyone. I wanted to experience flirting with boys I liked, and having them like me back, but my shyness would not let that happen. I was missing the most fun part of being a teenager.

Chapter 7: Junior High

I enjoyed my eighth-grade year. Changing classes was exciting for me. I didn't get bored being stuck in the same room all day with the same teacher. I had secret crushes on two boys that I thought were cute. I loved being in the same art class with both of them. I mostly hung out with a couple of girls who weren't very popular. I knew they were not popular, but it didn't matter. I felt comfortable with them. I sat with them in art, where I could find joy in drawing and in watching the boys I liked.

In eighth grade a few people were shorter than I, and I loved that. This was also the year I got contacts. I have brown eyes with long eyelashes. Once I got used to seeing my eyes without thick glasses over them, I started to see that I was actually pretty. My eyes were my best feature, and they were no longer hidden. The first day I wore those contacts, my English teacher said, "I like your new eyes."

Sometimes I hung out with a red-haired, freckled girl named Kim from the trailer court near my house. She wasn't very stylish or clean, and the others didn't like her much. Neither did I, really, but I was always nice to her. She sometimes came over to my house to ask for shampoo or panty hose, and even pads one time, because she needed them and her mother hadn't provided them.

The first day I got my contacts, Kim told me my face looked weird without glasses. That embarrassed me a little. Another time she said, "You know, you're really pretty. You could be popular if you wanted to be." I didn't know if I should take that as a compliment or not.

Even in eighth grade it was difficult for me to ask questions in class. In science class one day, I wanted to know what form of matter fire was. I pushed past my shyness and raised my hand to ask. It was so hard. My heart was beating fast and my breathing was shallow and quick. But I did it, and I was proud because it was a good question that stumped the teacher at first. He answered my question and my curiosity was satisfied. It felt good to be able to express myself a little. Too bad it had to be so difficult.

Chapter 8: High School

The best part about Hillcrest High School was that I met my good friend Rachel. She and I are still friends. I don't remember this, probably because I didn't realize it, but she says she kept talking to me and trying to be my friend, but that I wouldn't talk to her. God bless her for her persistence. If it hadn't been for that, I may have been friendless. I hung out with Rachel and a girl named Rhonda, but Rachel was the glue between Rhonda and me. So I had a couple of friends.

I had always wanted to be a Highlander, my school's drum and bugle corps, but I didn't have the confidence to try out. Fortunately, Rachel talked me into trying out, and we both made it. It was fun being involved like that.

I had a crush on Kevin, a boy from school, all four years. His cousin Kristen was in my English class, and she was always pushing him to ask me out. I never told anyone I liked Kevin, but she must have sensed it. He finally told her he wasn't going to ask me out, because I was too quiet. I felt broken because I liked him so much, and I was missing out on the fun, again.

Chapter 9: Pyrophobia

I was afraid of more than just people as a child. I was also afraid of fire. When I was very small, we rented an old white house in the country. My mother was in the kitchen, holding me on her hip while she cooked. When she opened the old oven, it exploded heat and a deep horrible noise into our faces.

Then when I was two or three years old, we had a house fire. An ugly naked light bulb started it. The fire ran up the thick white bedroom curtains. Frightened, I followed my grandmother around the house as she soaked a heavy blanket in the bathtub, and then returned to cover the fire with the wet blanket over and over again. When the fire finally died, we dropped onto the sofa, shaking with relief and exhaustion. "Aqui estan tus hijos," ("Here are your children,") she sighed dramatically when Mom and Daddy came home. I always wondered why she didn't get us out and call the fire department instead.

That house fire was probably what started my intense fear of fire. After that, there were many incidents when I was irrationally afraid of it, such as the time when one of my siblings had a birthday, and I hid in my bedroom just because my mom lit the birthday candles on the cake. It was humiliating.

That fear followed me around, even in church. Children's church wasn't supposed to be traumatic. I don't even remember the point of the object lesson the day we had a special speaker who could do magic tricks. But I will never forget the stiffening fear as the evangelist lit the flame that represented something biblical. From then on I thought twice about sitting on the front row anywhere.

Then there was that August day at the circus. People take children to the circus to amuse them, but I hated the circus because the circus had clowns, and clowns always lit firecrackers. It didn't matter that the Kool-Aid man was there. I didn't care about the cold but tasty popcorn in the red and white striped boxes. The show dogs with their little skirts lost their appeal because firecrackers reminded me of fire. I sat as close to Mom as I could, fanning away the cigarette smoke with my baby sister's diaper.

Cigarettes scared me too, because they had fire. Once I was buried in a crowd at Tiffany's bakery, and a woman burned my nose with her cigarette. I had the scar for years. The scrawny woman was wearing a faded black terry cloth short set. Her shoulders were bare, covered only by her stringy dirty hair. Her son stood close behind her, with his fists stuck in the front of his shirt at the chest. I can never forget the way those people looked as the woman halfheartedly said in her whiny voice, "Oh, I'm sorry. Are you OK?"

Once when I was twelve, we were driving on the highway and traffic was not moving. There was a small red car on the side of the road next to us, in flames. "Hurry! Drive in the turning lane! It's going to explode!" I screamed, feeling helpless and trapped. It was not until several decades later that I realized that my two biggest fears were related.

Chapter 10: The Quiet College Freshman

If it hadn't been for the constant overwhelming anxiety, my college years would have been some of the best years of my life. But college is when you decide on a career and a life partner. Looking back now, I realize I wasn't prepared to decide on either of those.

After graduating from high school, I enrolled in college, because my father taught there, and tuition would be free. It was assumed that I would go to college, and truly I wanted to go, but what I needed first was therapy.

I kept a journal through my college years, and nothing tells the story better than that journal.

6-29-90
I can't believe I'm going to be in college! It seems a little silly to live in the dorms when I have a house right here, but lots of Greenville people do it. They say you fit in better and you have more fun. But I'm dying! Who am I going to room with? I can't imagine being put with someone I don't even know. What if we don't like each other? What if they're scary?

9-21-90
Well, Daddy arranged for me to room with one of his students, a Spanish major two years older than me, named Stephanie. She's a complete stranger to me, but at least Daddy knows her, which helps

some. I got to the dorm a few days before Stephanie did. I moved all my stuff in: my black and white comforter, my plush Minnie Mouse, a big poster of a black panther by a grand piano, and a few clothes. This was my first time out of the house, and it was exciting going from my old pink bedroom at home to my new black and white college dorm room.

9-25-90

I attended all my freshman orientation meetings, and on the third day, my roommate arrived. I was in my room when I heard a key in the door, and in walked Stephanie, a tall and big boned, but not fat, 20-year-old. She had shoulder-length, straight brown hair. She seemed confident and sure of herself, and was a little intimidating to me. But I liked her.

We introduced ourselves and told each other our major. I spoke softly. I was nervous. But Stephanie was talkative, which helped break the ice. She told me all about her trip to Peru, and the man she had met there and almost married. She began unpacking her belongings, which included a South American wall hanging and quilt for her bed, and a few knickknacks. I can see she's not into the sleek black and white look I'm going for, but it doesn't matter. She has her half of the room; I have mine.

I can see too that we're going to be different from each other. When she introduced me to her friends and our suite mates, I felt like I would not fit in. There is Becky, a petite, dark and curly-haired girl from the south; and Melinda, a blond, funny, overweight girl who is majoring in music. They're both very outgoing. All three of them love to laugh. I feel a little left out because they're all upperclassmen. They try to include me, but I'm too shy.

9-27-90

My first semester of college classes has started and it's hot! We actually have class in some old World War II era barracks. There's no air conditioning, and we're not allowed to wear shorts. What a stupid rule! Who are they to tell me what I can wear? Is it a sin to show my knees? I'm sweating through my classes, literally but not figuratively. Academics have always been my strength. But socializing has always been my weakness. I don't understand myself; I just hate myself.

Today after listening to a chapel speaker preach that shyness is of the devil, I trudged back to my dorm feeling sad. The preacher seems to think that only outgoing, talkative, aggressive people can "witness."

10-5-90
My roommate talked me into going street witnessing. I was scared and could not talk. I promised myself that if I went again, I would not be shy. I do wish I could be a "better Christian witness," but I'm a pretty eighteen-year-old in a college full of young guys, with my life ahead of me. I want to overcome my shyness so I can have some fun!

12-9-90
Melinda told me at lunch today that she was talking to some guys who wish that I would open up more and not be so quiet. That must be why nobody asks me out. They can't see my personality, because I'm too shy. I hate it.

1-1-91
My first New Year's Eve midnight as a college student was spent sitting on my bed by myself crying, and wishing myself a Happy New Year.

2-17-91
I like this tall, thin, brown-haired guy with a charming smile who is in my math class. He's popular with girls for his cuteness and his friendliness. I get giddy whenever he talks to me. It must be obvious that I like him, but I've never told anyone. How do I let him know I'm interested? He's friendly; I'm the problem. I think he could be interested in me if I weren't so shy. I'm missing out on the fun!

3-15-91
Last night Stephanie and I were listening to 50s and 60s music in our room. She was dancing, and I was just sitting on the bed eating a sucker. She said, "Susanna, you have to dance or you can't be my roommate next year." Then she told me about how much fun she and Becky had dancing wildly. It made me feel so boring.

4-9-91
Becky decided not to return to school next year. She said to Stephanie, "You're gonna miss me. Susanna won't be able to make you laugh until you cry like I do. She'll just sit and look at you." That hurt.

5-26-91
If I could change anything about my past, it would be the fact that I wouldn't talk in school when I was little. That memory is so embarrassing for me. Why was I so weird? I wonder if what the psychiatrist told my parents is true, that I was just being stubborn and refusing to talk.

Chapter 11: A Doctor?

It was a hot Wednesday in July. Everyone was drippy and cranky. I had spent the day at home reading, and I thought it would be a good idea to go to church that evening to air myself out and maybe get some encouragement. After the meeting I drove home and came into the kitchen, unaware of what I was walking into.

"How was church tonight?" asked Mom in a flat voice.

I answered, "Every time I go to the college group I get depressed. I don't talk to anybody, so no one talks to me."

"Why don't you talk to anyone then?" she asked accusingly.

"Because I'm so shy, lonely, and boring. That's why!" I snarled, almost in tears.

Mom got furious, again. "At home, you kids are different than you are with other people. Outside of the house you're just mousy little things, doing what everybody else tells you to do. But here at home, you're disrespectful and rude!"

I could tell something had been going on at home to make Mom so irritable. Then I noticed my sister crying. Oh. So they must have been fighting, and then I walked in and announced a problem that had gnawed at our family for as long as I'd been around—my crippling, profound shyness. I hated myself for it. I resolved to try to do better and force myself to talk and stand up for myself. Feeling my chest hurt and my arms numb over, I went to my room and slammed the door. A picture fell off the wall. I kicked it aside and fell into bed, the warmth of the waterbed lulling me into a numb, light sleep.

7-10-91
I do not like this world any longer. I can't wait to leave for Heaven. I
hurt so much inside. I don't like myself. I'm stupid and weird. Tonight
I got so upset that I cried. It's a good thing it was night, and too dark
for anyone to see my tears.

Since I had spent my summer daydreaming about how much fun
it would be to be a pediatrician, I decided to be pre-med. I declared a
Biology major with a Spanish minor, and I signed up for pre-med classes
like biology and chemistry.

My freshman year roommate, Stephanie, decided she wanted her own
room, so I had to either find a new roommate myself, or the college would
assign me one. I wasn't about to take that risk, so I asked a friend to room
with me, and to my pleasant surprise, she said yes. Her name was Grace,
and she was studying to be a nurse. Tall and friendly, she was a great
roommate. My only complaint was her good intentions to go running at
5 a.m., which was really a constant snoozing of the alarm clock until I
was good and awake, and annoyed. Other than that she was my favorite
roommate.

Through Grace I met Tim, a cute, friendly boy with shoulder-length
blond hair, not too tall, who was majoring in biology. One January evening
he came by our room presumably to talk to Grace about a class assignment
they both had. I was sitting at my desk studying. Every time I looked up,
Tim's eyes were looking at me, even though he was talking to Grace.

"Hi," Tim said to me.

I blushed and said, "Hi," then looked back at my chemistry book.

When Tim finished visiting with Grace, he left, and Grace said to me,
"He likes you."

"No he doesn't," I replied. But really I felt giddy and happy and very
excited. I think Tim might have asked me out had I not been so incredibly
shy around him. I just couldn't talk. I missed out again.

In the spring I went on a Medical Missions trip to Mexico. I was an
interpreter for the doctors and nurses and their patients. It was awesome.
On that trip I met a guy named Dan. We became friends, often doing
things together, but I didn't "like-like" him. Something, to this day I
don't know what, always kept me from romantic feelings with people I was
actually friends with. It seemed I only liked those I couldn't have. So one
Sunday in December, Mom asked me if I liked my friend romantically. I
told her I didn't, because even though I had tried, I just couldn't. She said

I would end up like her cousin, who never married because she just kept waiting for a perfect love to happen. I felt doomed.

I was often lonely for whole days at a time, sometimes eating every single meal alone. I barely spoke to anyone. In addition to my shyness, insomnia wove its way through my days and nights. I couldn't stand the feeling of being tired but not sleepy.

And on top of that, I was beginning to have doubts about becoming a doctor. I was way too anxious about it, and I wondered if doing something else would bring me peace.

2-20-92
I can only stick to one major for two semesters. I hate this. I wish I knew what to do. I hate going back and forth so much. I can't be a teacher because of my terror of public speaking. I have to overcome my stage fright! I can no longer live with this overwhelming burden. It has ruined my life.

Chapter 12: A Spanish Teacher?

6-19-92
My summer is filled with insomnia, and devoid of a social life. All I want is to be able to carry a good conversation! But that's elusive. I simply don't have the skills. I'm sick of being me. Shy little me, always worried about how I come across in conversations. Confused, weak little me in thick heavy glasses or itchy contacts. Me with my ever-present eczema rash. I have no personality, I am dull, and I don't know how to have fun. Everything bores me, and I bore everyone. I can't make decisions. I wonder if I need a shrink.

7-26-92
It's 4 a.m. and I am completely wide awake.

Grace graduated, so once again I needed a new roommate for my junior year. A girl named Alicia asked me to be her roommate, and I accepted. An elementary education major, friendly, outgoing Alicia was a nice girl and fun to be around. But she was hard to live with. She was messy. Also she stayed up late making noise, but when she was sleeping until noon on Saturdays, she expected me to be quiet for her.

For my junior year I was a Spanish major. I felt a little more relaxed that year, but sadly I couldn't get excited about my decision to be a Spanish teacher. I kept wishing I were pre-med, but I couldn't feel totally happy with that choice either. I was a little depressed because nothing in life excited me. I just sat and worried a lot.

One night in January, the most depressing month of the year, my roommate had a party at her parents' house. Alicia's parents lived in a nice big house surrounded by trees. The bedrooms were upstairs, where her parents remained, and we had the run of the whole downstairs for the party. The house was very clean. Only the ill-mannered black and white pug dog bothered us with her yipping and snapping. I couldn't stand that dog, but I gravitated toward it. Petting the dog made me feel more comfortable, because it was less obvious that I wasn't talking to anyone.

"Help yourselves to snacks and drinks," announced Alicia.

I spent quite a bit of time at the snack table, slowly sipping my drink and eating cookies and chips. It was something to do besides sit there and look at people, and it made me feel a little bit less self-conscious. Everyone around me was mingling. I caught snatches of this conversation and that one. Even those who weren't particularly outgoing were having a better time than I. I didn't feel like I socialized at all. I certainly didn't carry on any sparkling conversations, killing any potential ones in the first few minutes.

Alicia and her potential boyfriend walked past me sitting on a carpeted step.

"Mingle," said Alicia, and gave me a smile. "Try not to be shy." A few minutes later she introduced me to a curly redheaded guy.

"This is Jake," she said. "Jake, this is my roommate, Susanna. Jake is a biology major."

"Hi," I said.

"Nice to meet you," said Jake. "Where are you from?"

"Greenville," I answered. "Where are you from?"

"I come from Michigan. I heard the biology program here was good, and I want to be an optometrist."

I nodded, having a hard time making myself heard above the music.

"What's your major?" Jake asked me, just to keep the conversation going. That question again! Why did everyone have to ask, "What's your major?"

"I was a biology major, but I changed it to Spanish."

"Isn't your dad the Spanish teacher here?"

"Yes, Dr. Castro."

"How is your Spanish grade?" he asked with a teasing smile.

"Pretty good," I said, trying to smile but my lips were shaking too much.

Then there was an awkward silence, and Jake said, "Well, it was nice to meet you."

"Nice to meet you too," I muttered. And Jake went to join a group of people chatting and laughing on the couch.

Of course he wants to talk to someone more fun and interesting, I thought. As the party got going, conversations got more animated, people began playing card games, and someone turned on a movie in one corner of the living room. I sat there to watch, until, yawning, I went home to our dorm at eleven.

I felt terrible about myself after that party, so embarrassed and sad. Knowing Alicia probably wouldn't be back for a while, I sat up in bed to write in my journal:

1-16-93
I'm in a horrible mood. I'm being totally boring. I wish I could make something fun and exciting happen, but I'm too dull. I guess I'll just go to bed. I wish I didn't have to get up tomorrow at all.

I was always complaining, always moping, always depressed.

2-26-93
I feel really sad because I hardly ever talk. I feel boring. Alicia told me I looked bored. I felt so bad tonight. I hardly talked at all! I never do! That always plagues me, all my life. I wish I were more fun. I always just sit and blink. I'm sad.

I had to make a presentation in my English class. Three or four people went before me, and the whole time they were speaking I was nervous. My hands were cold. My guts were churning. My breathing was shallow. I dreaded my turn, but I wanted it to come so I could get it over with. Finally, it was my turn. I walked to the front of the room. With shaky knees and nothing but a low table to lean on, I began talking, but I kept gulping and my lips were shaking. My voice was shaky too, and I spoke too fast and quiet. My discomfort was so great that I ended up cutting my speech short and sitting back down. It was so embarrassing.

3-29-93
I despise being shy. I made an utter fool of myself today in my English presentation. I feel like killing myself. I hate life. I wish the Lord would return. I am angry and embarrassed.

4-14-93
I feel nervous right now. There is absolutely no reason to be nervous, but I can't help it.

4-21-93
I'm not excited about my future. In fact, I'm scared. I'm too nervous a person to have a career. Sometimes I just want to die, in spite of the fact that I love life.

5-8-93
I have so much free time that my brain gets bored. I start repeating meaningless syllables over and over like a crazy woman.

5-18-93
It seems like I am miserable all the time these days.

5-19-93
I have been having such a hard time sleeping and eating lately. I hate it. For example, today I am exhausted, but I can't sleep at all! Last night, I woke up at 4 a.m. And I hardly ever eat. Yesterday, I could barely force down a soft taco. I wish I weren't such a nervous person. It's quite ridiculous. I really do hate it.

5-22-93
I crave peace and joy. I have Jesus, but I do tend to worry a lot about what people are going to think of me. I hate that.

Chapter 13: Now What?

My senior year in college was my sister Monica's freshman year. I asked her to be my roommate, and she said yes. I thought that would be wonderful, since I love my sister, but it turned out to be hard because everyone wanted to be her friend, and no one seemed to want to be mine. She had such an easy way with people. She was popular; I was reclusive. I always felt on the fringe, which only hurt my failing self-esteem. I struggled with jealousy. Not in a malicious way; I was happy for my sister and wouldn't have changed her life. I just wished I too could have the personality and social skills she had. It was hard always having to watch someone else so close to me have what I wanted so badly: friends and a life.

I finished my Spanish major and Biology minor the first semester of my senior year, but for lack of anything better to do, I stayed another semester just taking classes.

In all my life I had never felt so low. I felt I had absolutely no ambitions or callings on my life, and I felt stupid. What was I going to do? I didn't fit in anywhere and I hated life.

1-23-94
I am not happy. I'm graduating, and I don't know what I'm going to do. I don't know how to find a job. I applied at ten different places, and didn't get hired. My whole life has been full of failure in that area, and I'm tired of being completely dependent on my parents.

5-8-94

Tomorrow I'm going to be more sociable and call my friends. I feel kind of sad because I'm growing older and I haven't met a man I really want to date. I hope I do soon.

Chapter 14: A College Graduate

I couldn't believe I had just graduated from college! It was shocking how fast my college years went by. The Saturday after graduation, I woke up feeling very depressed and let down, like after the holidays when all you have is wet gray slush outside and cold, cold darkness. Graduation day was cozy and wonderful, full of family and friends, gifts and good wishes. But the next morning, everything stretched empty and lifeless in front of me. Feeling sad but unable to cry, I got ready for my $4.50/hour job at Heer's department store downtown.

Impatient for something to do full time that sounded good enough, I took on a missionary assignment with an office that produced children's curriculum for missionaries to use in Latin America. It sounded good, but it turned out to be the worst thing. I cringe with embarrassment when I think of it: I actually sent letters to people, asking them for financial support while I volunteered! I barely got any support, so the missionary lady in charge of the office gave me some of her support. I did the most boring, tedious work ever—filing and data entry. I hated it. The people I worked with were nice—I liked them, but the highlight of my day was walking to the post office to get the day's mail. I lived for the weekends. One time I actually fell to my knees, because I was so glad the week was over.

I was jealous of my two younger sisters, who seemed to have it all together—beauty, intelligence, a lot of friends, a social life, jobs they liked, and school. I wanted to be just like them.

On many mornings I woke up ridiculously early, extremely anxious and unable to sleep. Sometimes I couldn't even eat very much. I wished I could cry to get the tension out, but I couldn't. I couldn't relax. I hated it when I couldn't sleep when I had the opportunity, and then I felt tired at the wrong times. How I wished I could cry and sleep and be happy. But all I could do was worry for an unexplainable reason.

In February 1995 I had a big decision to make. My boss wanted me to keep my missionary assignment for a long time. I had planned to leave in August, after one year. But she offered to pay me more money, and I felt pressured. She didn't want to find someone to replace me, because someone else would take a long time to learn the job and be productive. And I had done so much already.

I fretted over the decision. I made a pros and cons list. I worried about what God wanted me to do, and about how I just wanted to do the right thing.

Finally, because I was frustrated with my job and felt like I wasn't being challenged, I decided to leave in August as I had originally planned.

Chapter 15: The Dark Days

6-1-95
Mom hurt my feelings deeply. She told me my life was pathetic. I'm doing my best! I really am! My feelings were hurt so badly that my body physically hurt. Well, there's truth in her statement. I'm not going anywhere.

8-7-95
I want to get married. I want companionship and a family. I hope I'm not being like Scarlett O'Hara, longing for something I cannot have, and overlooking and rejecting a great blessing. I need God's help!

I got a job at Cox South hospital as a Nursing Administration secretary. That job was great. There was plenty of variety, which I needed. It was not predictable. And I was happy with the pay, which is much more than I can say for my previous job. But I was only a part-time secretary. I needed to do more.

I had never really lost my interest in the medical field, so I decided that while I was working at Cox, I would go back to school for some more science classes, try to get a job in the medical field to get some experience, and then apply to physician's assistant school.

While taking my science classes, I had a job interview with St. John's cardiovascular unit. The job sounded very interesting. Mostly I would have taken arterial samples. I really didn't think that would bother me, but the interviewer kept planting doubts in my mind about going into a medical career. I felt terrible, and wondered if maybe I should have gone back to school for an elementary teaching degree instead. I was very upset with myself for being so nervous. I could hardly talk, and later I kept thinking of all the things I could have said. I wanted that job so badly, but I was just so scared.

8-30-95
My only doubt about trying to become a physician's assistant is: what if blood bothers me? But I can get used to that. I just want so badly to know for sure what is for me. I go through my cycle of doubts and I despise that. I am 23 years old and I have been out of college a year. I'm going back to school tomorrow to study for something I thought I wanted, but I'm not sure now. It's just that the thought of elementary education keeps popping into my mind. But I have doubts about that too. I have doubts about everything. Nothing is sure and perfect for me.

During those confusing, dark days I wondered if I would ever get my life going. I knew I was stuck, but I didn't know why. I felt torn apart, lost, and humiliated. I needed peace.

9-8-95
Most Friday nights I just sit at home alone. I have to go to church because it's my only social life. I go out after church because everyone is invited. At least I have that. I'm having career problems. I have no dates, and very few friends.

This was the truth of my life all those years, but in spite of it I often felt content. Whether it was because I had just learned to exist that way and didn't know better, or because God was carrying me through, or both, I don't know.

9-10-95
I'm still dealing with my general anxiety attacks. I wake up too early, and feel adrenaline coursing through my body. I get butterflies in my stomach.

9-16-95
Another Saturday night at home, as usual. I really wish I could get out more. I miss having friends around all the time. Even in the dorms I was lonely sometimes, but it's nothing like it is now. At least in college

I went out every weekend. Now I always stay home. I wonder when it will end. When will I ever have a date? How soon will this lifestyle change? I can't imagine going out with a group of friends, or dating, or getting married and having children. I feel like I want so much to advance in life, but I can't because I'm stuck.

11-25-95
I feel a little cranky this morning. I'm tired, but I woke up anyway, before I got my rest.

12-1-95
I can see myself as the oldest daughter who never married. I am sad and lonely again. Yet another weekend spent home alone, without even my family. I want to cry, but I can't. I wonder why I live? What am I good for anyway? I hate even thinking about a career. It's been nothing but a nightmare for 6 years, and I've had it.

12-22-95
I am so depressed today! I could just cry. It's Friday night, and I'm home alone, again. I need to learn to make plans ahead of time. I like to keep busy. That way I don't feel the loneliness as much. It's been this way all my life, but it's been worse ever since I graduated from college. I'm making cupcakes, and escaping to the mall. This is a bad and expensive habit, but I'm going to buy myself something both to entertain myself and to ease the pain of loneliness and boredom. Sometimes I wish I could go to sleep and never wake up.

1-5-96
I have always tried to act cool when I like someone, because I never want to be teased. But mostly I don't want anyone to see that I've been rejected and disappointed. I wonder what ruined me.

1-16-96
Life really hurts. I'm crying, because of the pointlessness of it all. These are tears of loneliness and boredom. My heart is broken, because all my life I have been a nobody. I'm not fun. I'm shy and awkward, and I'm not good at anything. I cry almost every night.

While I was working part-time at Cox hospital and taking science classes, I applied at several physician's assistant programs in the country. I got one interview, in New Jersey. I was thrilled. I thought maybe I was finally going somewhere. Maybe I would have the medical career I dreamed of after all. I wanted this so badly.

I asked for time off work, and Mom and I drove to New Jersey for the interview. When we finally arrived, exhausted and hungry after two days of driving, we stopped at Boston Market for some chicken and some buttery side dishes. Then we went to our relatives' dirty house in a bad neighborhood, where we did not feel at home. They set us up in a bedroom that was really just a curtained-off part of the living room, on a couple of thin mattresses on the floor. The bathroom was brown with dirt and there was hair in the sink. The mirror was broken and there was hardly enough room to turn around. Our cousins might as well have been strangers to me—it had been so long since I'd seen them. But I tried to be positive, since this would be my closest link to home, if I got accepted at the school.

The morning of the interview we set off early, to be sure we didn't get lost. It's a good thing we did, since it took us a while to find the right building. They were conducting the interviews in a white trailer. The room was full of prospective students, all of them more qualified than I. Most of them had been working in the medical field in some capacity, and were not from out of state. I figured my biggest strike against me was that I was from out of state. Perhaps, but ultimately it may have been my extreme anxiety that shut that door for me. I was so nervous I couldn't even talk straight. I stammered and gulped a lot. I could hardly get the words out. After the very short interview, I told my mom how badly I had spoken and how embarrassed I felt. But what could we do? It was over, and there was nothing left to do but drive back home.

A few weeks later when they told me they couldn't offer me a place in the physician's assistant program, I was crushed. So I had another decision to make. I could keep trying, or I could go with my other idea—to become an elementary school teacher.

I decided to return to school, this time for elementary education. That was a bad idea! The education classes were too easy and I missed the intellectual challenge of my science and foreign language classes. I did well academically, but I was terrible at teaching. When I got up in front of a class to teach, I got so nervous that my mouth trembled and my voice shook. I kept gulping air. It was extremely embarrassing. My practicum teachers tried to be positive. But I really was bad at managing my class.

When I did my student teaching, my poor supervising teacher had a hard job training me. I'm embarrassed when I think back to my teaching days.

I wrote in my journal a lot when I was going through hard times. Here are some entries:

11-6-96
Pain of the emotions makes you feel numb, and your arms and legs hurt dully. It's lead and electrical sparks. It's slowness, a wavering mirage of the world and who you are. The picture blurs, and you hurt.

1-13-97
I'm nervous tonight because tomorrow I start a new practicum, in the classroom where I'm doing my student teaching. I really don't like teaching. I hate feeling nervous. I don't like to feel like I'm going to throw up, or cry. I hate the embarrassed feeling of knowing my mouth is trembling and my nervousness shows. The kids will see it, and take advantage of it. I'm praying for self-confidence and calm tomorrow.

5-4-97
It seems that I am never completely happy and carefree. I have been happy only a few short times in my life. I have to always worry about one thing or another. I hate it! Why can't I be a sunnier person? I want to be a child again, but not go to school. My childhood summers were the happiest times of my life.

5-14-97
I've been very frustrated lately. I messed up a very good chance at a job. I was too nervous at my first interview, and I didn't even ask many questions! I feel terrible. I wonder if I have psychiatric problems.

5-27-97
I feel like a hopeless little failure. What will my future be like? I can't find a job, and I can't imagine finding my dream job, ever. I'm more patient now than before, but I still worry. I feel trapped in my parents' home. I never have a date. And today, I found another white hair.

5-29-97
Every time I see a romantic movie, I get sad, depressed, and jealous.
I feel lonelier than ever. I can't imagine ever finding anyone myself.
I want marriage and children more than anything else in the world.
But I can't because I'm too shy. I feel like I'm wasting my young, pretty
years sitting at home alone. I'm really worried about my future, but
there's nobody to talk to about it. I can barely see through my tears.
I'm so sad I can't even force a smile.

Chapter 16: The Biggest Failure

The biggest failure of my life came with my first (and last) teaching job. The day I took the job I regretted it. But since it was my last opportunity, I went ahead and took it. This was my chance to wander, to realize a dream. But it was horrible. First of all, the principal interviewed me over the phone. I don't think I would have gotten the job if I had interviewed in person. I would have trembled and faltered my way out of the job. But I would soon find out how desperate they were for a new teacher, because they offered me the job and I accepted. I would be teaching first grade at Pecan Grove Elementary School in Yuma, Arizona. Pecan Grove had a lot of students, and it was a difficult school in a rough neighborhood. Plus it had a new bilingual program, an added challenge I did not need.

My mom and I had decided to drive to Arizona together, and then she would fly back home. We tried to forget about the fact that I was leaving home, and just enjoy the trip like a vacation.

The morning I was to leave for my new life, I absolutely could not sleep. I didn't feel well at all. We packed my long blue Oldsmobile with our things—suitcases filled with clothes, and boxes of books and teaching supplies. The whole back seat was taken up with stuff.

Mom had promised to "be good" and not cry, and not tell me that I was making a mistake. And she kept her promise. She was very "good." We both were doing our best to cover up our feelings. But we genuinely enjoyed each other's company.

We headed west and drove all day across Oklahoma. When we hit New Mexico that evening, I started to get really excited. The sky was a darkly brilliant blue. Lightning flashed behind the mesas.

At night we stopped at a Motel 6. We had everything we needed there. We enjoyed the swimming pool. But when they closed the pool early that night, there was that much more time to worry. I slept very little. And I couldn't eat. I had to force food down. I was nervous and didn't have much of an appetite.

The next day, the hours in the car blurred together as we passed them listening to a LeAnn Rimes tape before accidentally melting it in the car. The most exciting moment of our trip was when we crossed the Arizona state line. We happened to be listening to The Eagles. There's the song about Winslow, Arizona, and the Indian music in "Witchy Woman." I saw the red rocks, the brown topography with tufts of dry green bushes, the mesas, and the same lightning. It rained lightly as I drove through an Indian reservation for the first time. Navajo. I was actually glad I came. I wanted to laugh.

On the second day we took a northward detour to the Grand Canyon. Mom took me to a steakhouse for dinner. The décor was dark and Western. They had an eating contest going on. Diners who could eat a 72-ounce steak in one sitting got their steaks for free. The tables were full of pretty people, happy in their new clothes bought just for their Grand Canyon trips. It was a great place, but my throat closed up and the knots in my stomach would not let me enjoy the food. I forced down some fat Texas toast, pretended to enjoy a cut of meat, and gratefully gulped a glass of iced tea to help it go down. I was so scared about my new job and new life. I realized then that I really didn't want to be there. Mom and I tried to enjoy ourselves as we talked about everything but our thoughts. I was trying to be brave, but I kept thinking, "What will it be like? What if I hate it?"

I knew Mom was thinking, "What if she never comes home?"

My mind wouldn't let go of "What have I done?" It kept playing over and over: "What have I done? Why am I here? What did I do?"

That evening we checked into a beautiful Quality Inn. After soaking in the hot tub for a while, I thought, "I look good in my swimsuit!" I wanted to talk to the young guys there, but I just couldn't. "I have to stop this! I have to stop being this shy!" I thought. As if I could.

I didn't think about it at all at the Grand Canyon. Instead, the foreign, expansive red beauty swallowed us up. We were taxed by the hike and happy. But the recording in my mind started again and got louder as we drove into the desert, the Gila Mountains hissing at us in the distance. "What have I done?"

Yuma, a military desert town, is in the southwest corner of Arizona, so we still had a lot of driving to do. As we drove through the desert, we began to realize that we should have gotten gas while we still could. By then there was nothing but the heat and many miles of desert. Our anxiety grew as the road stretched in front of us and there was still no gas station in sight. The gas gauge was dipping ever closer to empty. We were silently praying that we wouldn't run out of gas out there, two women alone, so far from home.

We didn't run out of gas. We finally found a gas station in town and filled up. When I opened the car door, my relief was replaced by a drop-off feeling as the desert heat hit my face. It was an oven. It actually hurt. "I have made the biggest mistake of my life," I thought. But it was interesting to see the "Beware of Rattlesnakes" sign. I took a picture and we quickly got into the car before we actually saw any rattlesnakes.

We arrived in Yuma in the evening. The first thing we did was look for a mechanic who could tell us why the "check engine" light was on. We learned that the cover to something was not put on right, but there was nothing wrong with my car. That was actually a miracle—we drove the whole way, 1,400 miles through the desert, without even putting water in! The pleasant mechanic who looked under the hood didn't even charge us.

As the sun set that evening, I started to see the beauty of the desert. The sky was brightly colorful, streaked orange, blue, purple, and yellow. When it got dark and the stars came out, I could see how close and abundant they looked. It was awesome. But still, my overriding emotion was nervousness. I was tense and anxious. I could not relax.

We followed the directions we had been given to the home of our friend Clara, who was going to let me stay with her until I got my own place. As we pulled up, I noticed that her yard was very different from mine at home. Instead of grass, she had sand! I couldn't believe it, but of course, what else would it be, in the desert? She welcomed us into her home, and as she and my mother are both very talkative, I had plenty of time with my thoughts.

I wanted to get my own apartment as soon as I could, because I was looking forward to setting up housekeeping and starting some normalcy. I was also dying to get into my classroom. I needed to get started setting up and making plans. But unfortunately, we found out the next day that they were doing construction and my classroom was not open yet. It was not open the next day either, or the next. By then I was really tense. I was frustrated and mad on top of the nervousness. This was not getting off to a good start. But what could I do?

Eventually the day came that my mother was to leave me in Yuma alone and fly back home without me. All I could think of was how scared I was. It didn't occur to me, or at least I didn't fully understand, how my mother must have felt. I am her firstborn, and I was moving farther than any of her children had ever done. And she knew, and deep inside I knew, that I was making a big mistake. I already didn't want to stay there, but I didn't have the guts to go back with her. I had to try. I had to follow through. So we did it. I took her to the airport, watched her get on the plane, and found myself alone. I imagine she finally allowed herself to cry. I tried not to cry, but I did.

Not wanting to go back to Clara's house until I felt more composed, I went to Yuma's tiny mall. I walked around crying silently and trying to control myself. When I got hungry, I bought myself a hot dog at Orange Julius. Nobody said anything about my tears, and I was glad. Finally, when there was nothing else to do and nowhere else to go, I went back to Clara's house. She saw me crying. I was not able to hide it after all.

Apartment hunting went well. I learned that I got there just in time, very close to too late. I got the summer rates on a nice apartment, which saved me about 200 dollars a month. The apartment building was very "southwest" in style, near a pretty neighborhood lined with palm trees. A few plants were forced to grow in front, with irrigation to keep them alive. The apartment was furnished with a small table and chairs, two couches, and a bed, nightstand, and dresser.

I had forgotten to call the electric company, so on my first night in my new apartment, I had no air conditioning and no electricity for lights or refrigeration. I spent the evening in the pool. Then I came in and sat around in a wet swimsuit, reading my teacher books by candlelight. It was cozy until bedtime, when all the novelty wore off. I could not sleep for hours because of the heat. I was desperate for electricity. Finally, I took a cold shower to cool myself off, and I fell into a hot sleep.

So my first night on my own wasn't fun, but the first full day was. This was the first time I ever set up housekeeping by myself, and I loved it! The highlight of my week was going to Big K to get supplies—food, laundry detergent, etc. I was so excited. I had a great time putting things away and setting up housekeeping. I went to a craft store for fall window clings and red-hot chili pepper lights for my kitchen. I enjoyed it thoroughly, but I still wished I were home. When I thought about home and how far away and alone I was, I couldn't even smile. I then began counting down the months until I could return home. Nine more months!

Finally, I got to set up my classroom. I hung the animal alphabet over the board, arranged the desks in groups of four, put posters on the walls, and set up my learning centers. My favorite learning center had little red and blue bears that the children used for counting and simple math. It was stressful, because there wasn't enough time to prepare. But what I was able to accomplish would have to do. Too soon, the first day of school arrived.

On my first morning as a first-grade teacher, I woke before dawn. For breakfast I ate a cup of strawberry yogurt, and as much of a bagel with cream cheese as I could swallow. I drove to school, where everyone was excited about the new year. It was hot; I had to make sure not to leave anything in the car that could melt.

"Hello! Good morning!" everyone called.

"Are you ready?" asked a veteran teacher.

"We'll see!" I said.

I carried my box of last-minute supplies to the classroom and set them down. Each minute was precious; I hadn't gotten to set up as early as I'd wanted to, and I didn't feel completely prepared. It wasn't long before the students started trickling in, some of them as scared as I was. One by one I greeted them and showed them their seats. At the suggestion of several experienced teachers, I had placed a coloring page on each desk, so the children would have something quiet to do when they arrived. But it did not keep them occupied as long as I thought it would.

I had decided to speak Spanish in the morning, and English in the afternoon. So the Spanish-speaking kids were comfortable that morning, while the English-speaking kids were not. All of them were quiet and hesitant at first. Where was the bad behavior I had been warned to expect? I began the day with a game, an icebreaker to make the students feel at ease. They were so shy! I almost didn't know what to do with that! But it didn't last long.

So the school year got underway. I began hating mornings because I would wake up at 5:30 and lie awake worrying and missing home. I couldn't cry. When I finally got up, I had to fight back tears of loneliness and homesickness. I despised the feeling and understood why it's called homesickness. You really do feel sick. It hurts, like all the wrong chemicals are coursing through your body. One time I even woke up trembling. I was anxious, and I couldn't eat very well.

I kept a journal pretty religiously:

8-19-97

I am miserable. I hate teaching. I don't have the personality for it. I can't control my kids. I don't know how to plan and teach. I want to go home! I have never felt so completely lost and overwhelmed in my whole life. I hate it.

8-26-97

I am really suffering here. You don't know how badly I wish I had stayed home. I should have listened to my gut feeling. What a mistake. There's nothing to look forward to except going home. All week I'm lost, confused, overwhelmed, frustrated, and scared. All weekend I'm lonely and homesick. I feel close to tears 90 percent of the time. I don't even enjoy the kids, and they're the reason I came! Jazmin's mother was mad this morning. She wants her in another class. My worst teaching nightmare has come true. I dread tomorrow. I know the kids will be wild from the beginning, and I won't have a chance to take attendance. I'll be harried all day long.

9-1-97

Life gets a little better in September. I saw rain today for the first time in a month. The weather is cooling down a bit. I've been supremely happy in my new apartment. Sunday morning I went to First Assembly of God, where we saw a movie about Jesus, and I met a new friend. We have a lot in common. I'm excited in hopes that a friendship develops. I love this Steinbeck quote: "with no recourse but to burst into tears and wait for death." I can either do that, or keep trying, in my new job.

9-5-97

I am excruciatingly lonely and sad. I want to go home.

9-12-97

I felt a little better when our team of first-grade teachers got together to plan. We had photocopies and a plan, and it seemed more organized and closer to what I needed as a first year teacher.

Jazmin is only six years old, but she wears lipstick and a little bra. She wears formal dresses to school a lot.

Poor Elizabeth had on a purple long sleeve velvet dress in the 106-degree heat. Some of the kids are so poor. Maybe she didn't have anything else to wear.

Maria is a little bully who struggles academically, but she's very sweet to me. Every day I get hugs and presents. The other day she brought me two strange fruits. I think they're pomegranates. I get lots of yucky candy that I pretend to eat.

I cry every time I remember how every kid wanted a different teacher.

I met Sarita at First Assembly. She noticed that I had walked in alone, so she slipped into the pew I was in and introduced herself. She was a few years older than I, and also single and living on her own away from home. Like me, she was bilingual and trying to get her career off the ground. Unlike me, she was relaxed, friendly, and outgoing. One Sunday she invited me to her house for a spaghetti lunch after church.

Sometimes we went to some other friends' house for dinner and a game of cards. One girl had a large happy dog that would go nuts anytime someone said anything that sounded like "go for," because she thought she was going to "go for" a walk. I enjoyed all that. It really kept me going. I was so glad I was able to find friends in Arizona. God is good. He did answer that prayer of mine.

My new friend Sarita was involved in some volunteer mission work. Every other Saturday the people of San Luis in Mexico brought their children to a Bible school provided by the Americans from across the border in Arizona. After the teaching and singing were over, everyone shared a meal in the little kitchen, eating in shifts for lack of space. Possibly the best meal of the week, it brought a lot of people to Saturday School. One Saturday Sarita invited me to join them.

San Luis was a depressing barrio, very flat and sandy. There was nothing but sky all around the broken shacks. This particular Saturday was cold and rainy. People huddled under the scant awning sheltering them from the cheerless work of El Niño, waiting. It was freezing, a sick kid vomited in the sand, and nobody knew who the toddler in the Christmas footie pajamas belonged to. But they were hungry, so they waited patiently in line to eat, the children first, the adults last. After the meal, the women stood in another long line for a head of lettuce and a small bundle of leftovers. Even though the food was strange and they didn't really like it, nothing was left on the plates. Every little scrap helps feed someone, and they were grateful.

One mother of too many, her extra weight bearing down on her flimsy house shoes, worried aloud to her friend about her surprise pregnancy.

"Estoy embarazada."

"Que Dios nos ayude."

The dusty children, some of them barefoot, sat in a semi-circle on some old tires, listening with interest to the Bible lesson, ragged from the morning's improvised relay races and Simon Says game. The lesson was long and boring, but they politely paid attention, all twenty-four of them. After story time, the children gathered with their parents in a circle to sing praises to God, accompanied by one badly tuned guitar. There was joy and a feeling of thankfulness in the songs, in spite of the poverty.

The fenced-in area where they held the meeting was surrounded by skinny, shivering dogs, begging for a scrap. It was pitiful to see the mother dog full of milk, shaking and staring inside. The small female with the cyst in her eye, the limping ones—all of them were hungry.

Then one of the dogs got inside the fence and in the middle of the circle of worshippers. Suddenly out of the crowd came a huge, silent, almost toothless old man with a winter cap on his head. With a giant bat he beat the dog on its back. The bat made a cracking sound and sent the poor little animal running with her tail between her legs, in terror, looking for an exit. She wanted to leave, but the fence was closed. All they had to do was open the fence and the dog would have left. Instead the singers turned into a mob, chasing the dog, screaming, and driving it crazy. It seemed like the chase was an eternal moment. I could not stop watching, and I could not watch. I hated the man with the bat, and the mob of children no longer seemed innocent. Finally the dog escaped, the people calmed down, and the singing resumed. But it seemed so stupid then. I had tears in my eyes for the dog, but I didn't feel for the people anymore.

That Saturday made my life richer. It was a break from my loneliness and failure. Although the incident with the dog did plant a small seed of cynicism in me, it was still so good to get my mind off my problems and myself for the day.

In late September they cancelled school because they were expecting Hurricane Nora to slam into the desert southwest. I was excited because I'd never been in a hurricane before. I never thought it would hit an arid desert town two hours inland. I made sure to park my car under the carport so it would be covered. I was relieved that I didn't have any pets to worry about.

The day they expected the hurricane, I woke up before daylight and immediately moved away from my window. I was nervous about the window blowing in. Since the ground couldn't absorb much water, people were using sandbags. It was exciting, not having to go to school, stocking up on batteries and bottled water. Then it was weird, because the rain just stopped. Hurricane Nora turned out to be just a tropical storm. It was nothing. We had school the next day.

9-25-97
I'm tired but not sleepy. I hate this uneasy early morning feeling I get when I wake up before light and think about my job. I feel better emotionally out here in the living room. I wonder why my room feels so bad? I wish I could sleep. My eyes are exhausted.

I had been looking forward to Thanksgiving Day for months because my brother Rafael was coming for a visit. I woke up excitedly at five that morning. The day dawned gray, the first cloudy day in a long time. But I didn't care, because I was going to cook my first Thanksgiving meal, and share my little place with someone.

But at seven, Rafael called to tell me that he had overslept and missed his flight. I got that awful sunken feeling of disappointment, the one where you feel hot and hollow. Bad news does that to me, but it only lasted a second. He was still coming, but I would have to wait. He got put on standby at the airport, and all I could do was hope he came soon.

I had fun grocery shopping, cleaning, and cooking by myself that day. In the evening I watched TV and made some learning centers for school. The dinner I was going to share with my brother turned out really well. The duckling was delicious and succulent. The cobbler could have been better, but it wasn't bad. I also had mousse; vegetables, including a cactus leaf; and Pillsbury dinner rolls. At least I could trust those. It was kind of sad how I set the table early, bought a new pitcher for our special drink, and cooked a great meal, only to nibble on it by myself and then put it away.

Finally Rafael arrived, and we had a wonderful visit. It was everything I had hoped for. After we ate our Thanksgiving dinner and slept a good night, we took off for San Diego, the most beautiful city with the most perfect weather ever. We disagreed a little—he's a night owl who wanted to experience the night life of San Diego; I'm a morning person who would prefer to get up early and see the touristy sights. We ended up going to Sea World, where Rafael complained until I lectured him. Overall it was a fabulous time. My brother gave me a great gift—something to look forward to, company in my loneliness, a break from the frightening routine of my new life, good fun, and warm memories. I was so grateful for his visit. It was hard letting go when it came to an end.

12-10-97
I woke up in the middle of the night. I am very nervous. I do this often.
I get anxious about normal days. Maybe I should see a counselor. I'm
a pretty unhappy person. Very anxious.

Things were so bad that I began considering quitting my teaching job and returning home. There was no pride in that, but there was no pride in how I was performing at work either. I went back and forth on it so many times. When I had an OK day, I wanted to stay and stick it out. When I had a horrible day, I was determined to quit at Christmas break.

It was not an easy decision, but toward the end of first semester I had already determined to leave. But just before I made that final decision, Mr. Montoya got a mentor teacher to help me get control of my classroom. She came and she was wonderful. She gave me some good suggestions, like when she told me I should arrange the desks in rows rather than in groups. She gave me hope, almost making me reconsider my still-recent decision to leave. Best of all, she encouraged me and made me feel like less of a failure.

So I did rearrange my desks to allow for less chatter and misbehavior from my students. I took her suggestions, but it was still too much for me. The homesickness combined with the difficult job snapped me into a final choice: for my sake and for the sake of my students, I chose to break my contract and go home.

I carefully wrote a resignation letter to my principal, who read it in front of me with a very serious expression on his face.

"Well, Susanna," he said, pronouncing my name in Spanish. "I certainly don't want you to be miserable."

He reminded me that it would be hard to get another teaching job if I broke this contract, and I said, "I know. I'm OK with that."

"OK. Thank you for telling me," he said.

"Thank you," I said, and feeling free but strangely sad, I went to lock up my classroom and go home for supper and lesson planning alone.

I called my family. Mom was overjoyed, glad that I was coming home. Daddy was glad that I had made a decision that would make me happy. But it would take a lot more than leaving my miserable job and coming home to my family to bring me happiness. For my problems came from a deep, dark place inside of me, a place that had not yet been found, much less understood.

12-17-97
I've suffered so much already, being as soft and sensitive as I am. What am I going to do now? What will I do? I have no job. Again. Ouch. I wish things had turned out better. I'm very sad. I need help. Badly. Ow.

12-20-97
Since I quit my job, I feel relieved, but sad. I miss the children already. I'm really going to miss my cozy, wonderful apartment, the palm trees, the stars, and being an independent woman. I miss being a first-grade teacher. That is, I miss the idea of it, not the actual work. On one hand, I'm glad I quit. I feel much more relaxed, like I did the right thing. But on the other hand, I am filled with regret. I was so unhappy there, but to quit midterm is pretty bad. There's no sense of accomplishment. I wish I were going back to a happy classroom. But it's not that way, and since it isn't, I would rather leave. I can't watch anymore the longing in my children's eyes as the other classes pass by, well taught and disciplined by excellent teachers. I can't watch disturbed children like Jazmin completely shut down and give up in misery, because I don't know how to deal with her. She and I have a lot in common. We both started in a big new school, lost, alone, and scared. With such a bad start, it's hard to turn things around. I was wounded every time one of my kids wanted another teacher. I couldn't take it anymore. I'm too sensitive. I take it personally.

12-26-97
I had a wonderful Christmas, so relaxed and hidden from my cares which surely lurk around the corner. But I hope this peace I feel lasts the rest of my life. I'll try to lay back and trust God.

12-28-97
I keep testing my wings, but I can't seem to fly.

Chapter 17: Job Hopping

After I moved back from Arizona, I worked at a temp agency and lived at home while saving money for eye surgery to cure my nearsightedness. Being able to see comfortably and clearly for the first time in almost twenty years was awesome!

One of my temp jobs was in an office that sold advertising. I filled in for the receptionist while she recovered from back surgery. My boss was a loud, round, short man with thinning brown hair and plastic glasses. He had a mustache but no beard. He was an all-business go-getter; a pushy, insensitive, but very happy, nerd.

I learned the office procedures and the computer pretty quickly, which impressed my boss. But he had one complaint about my work—the way I answered the phone. He said I was too quiet and shy when I answered. He lectured me about how I was the customers' first impression of his company, and I needed to sound more upbeat, friendly, lively, and confident. I could have taken that constructive criticism and tried to do better with my phone voice, but he actually stood over me, making me practice over and over how I was going to answer the phone. It was embarrassing! I felt like a cartoon, one who wanted to cry. I felt stupid.

In spite of everything, however, I enjoyed the job. The people were fun to talk to and the computer work wasn't bad at all. Also I loved getting an hour for lunch and going out for fast food. But it was a temp job, and temp jobs always end.

I was sad because I didn't have a job or a boyfriend. Mom hurt my feelings, almost more than anyone has ever done. She said, "Everyone else, all your friends and peers, are moving on. They have good jobs. They're getting married. And you're not." My whole body hurt when she said that.

I was crushed. Because I knew she was right. I wanted to change that, but I couldn't. She also often told me that I didn't want to get married. If I really wanted to, then I would have been married already. I told her that hurt my feelings, because I wanted to marry more than anything else, but I could not get a good relationship going.

3-15-98
I think I'm depressed. But I'm moving forward with life anyway. I refuse to stay in bed and mope. I did that last night, and it felt gross.

4-28-98
I cried a little when Isabel's boyfriend Mark came over and asked me, "Why are you not working?" I feel like I have to kill anyone who knows how I live, because I'm so embarrassed. I hate the way my life is going.

5-5-98
I am a stronger person for all the suffering I've been through. God does turn bad into good. Right?

5-6-98
I had laser vision correction surgery! I have 20/20 in both eyes! One of the best moments of my life was when the doctor took the bandage off my eye and I saw him clearly. I was so happy! My reaction must have been rewarding for him. I really appreciate this. Everything else in my life is going so badly, I really needed a positive. Thanks be to God.

5-20-98
I called a Christian counseling clinic. They can give me a discount, but I'm still not sure I can afford it. I have to pay the eye surgeon first. The thing is, it's a catch-22. I need a job with insurance to pay for this, but I will have a hard time finding a job until I can solve this shyness problem. Anyway, I know what they're going to say. Practice talking to people. I am, but it's still such a slow process.

Chapter 18: The Apartment for Spinsters

While I babysat for the Assemblies of God's School of Missions the summer after I got back from Arizona, someone who worked at Assemblies of God Headquarters told me she needed to hire an assistant editor. I interviewed for the job and got it! I was so happy because finally I would have enough money to live in my own apartment. I finally had a good full time job, something that had eluded me so far. And I thought the job would fit me, because all I would need to do was sit at a desk, more or less alone, and edit.

Since I finally had a good job, I could move into my own apartment! I chose to move into Columns IV. Then I had something happy to write about:

8-6-98
I'm slowly settling into my new apartment. It's cozy and feels like home already. I wish I could have been satisfied at home, so I could save money. But I'm happy here. With a swimming pool, hot tub, and tennis courts, you can't beat the back yard! I had so much fun tonight. My friend Rachel came over after work. She helped me decorate, then Monica came and we ate spaghetti. We all went swimming and sat in the hot tub. It's good to have my own place, and have people over. Thursday I get paid and we're going to Branson. I'm excited! And again, I'm so thankful for my new eyes.

But typically I was only in a writing mood when I was unhappy:

8-7-98
Mom's remark hurt. She said that people who want to get married do, and those who don't, it's because they don't want to. She says it's an attitude. I also got deeply sad when she told me that her friend says that Columns IV is the apartment complex for spinsters.

8-8-98
I'm so sad tonight, but I can't cry very much. I had my family over for supper, and I was fine and happy until Mark asked if I'd made any friends here yet. Then he asked me if any guys had talked to me. I know he doesn't mean to rub it in, but it makes me very sad. He always makes me feel like a shy, weird little reject. Then Isabel always says something about my shyness. Next time I'm going to tell Mark not to remind me. I might as well stop pretending I'm OK.

In the fall of 1998, Monica and I took a trip out west together. We drove to California, stopping and camping along the way. We saw beautiful fall scenery and enjoyed each other and our beautiful country. We met our brother Rafael in Las Vegas and had a great time there. I was happy and didn't cry, until it was time to drive home. As soon as we were on our way, driving on Highway 1 alongside the ocean, I began to cry. I just didn't want to go back to my life the way it was. My chest hurt again to think of it.

My emotional reaction to driving home from California made me realize that I needed to see a counselor. I could finally afford it, with my new health insurance. I got an appointment with Dr. Wolfe at the Burrell Center. I wrote about it in my journal:

8-15-98
My homework is to list five things that cause me fear, in order of severity, and do the easiest one. So in the next five weeks I have to initiate conversation with a new person. Dr. Wolfe talked a lot about my passivity. He said I'll be happier if I'm more assertive and positive. I'm used to living with sadness but I can live with joy. It's like Plato's people in the cave who came out into the blinding light. They went back into the cave because the light hurt their eyes too much. That's

how it is with me. It's going to be uncomfortable for a while, being sociable. But later I'll see how much better it is. Also, he thinks I may not really be shy, that I just learned it from my parents in a culture that doesn't fit the one around me. This was new to me. I cannot imagine myself not being shy, but it is wonderful to think that I could possibly break the habit, which is what he called it.

10-8-98
I feel so lonesome and unloving, seeing everyone around me falling in love. I'm left out. I hate reality. The fantasy world is much better. I'm learning that life is not as exciting as I thought it would be. That's so disappointing. I've been crying on and off all day. Even at brunch with a friend this morning, I felt upset. I could barely eat her delicious breakfast. There's just been this cloud of doom. Literally, my heart hurts.

10-10-98
Tonight I felt lonely. So lonely it hurt, and I forced out a few tears to try to ease the pain.

10-11-98
I had a much better day today, just being with people. But I am still going to die of a broken heart.

12-18-98
It's lonely coming home after work, cooking yourself a big dinner, then watching a movie alone. I hope I can keep up good spirits and stay busy with people, so I don't get bored and lonely. I hate those feelings.

Chapter 19: Depression

To this day I don't understand what my boss wanted that I wasn't doing. Things weren't going well at work and I knew it, so I began looking for a position in another department. I found an opening for an editor at a school for distance education, and got the job. I think for the first time in my life I beat someone at a job interview. It also helped that my dad worked there in the past. I really liked my job. The people were great and finally I fit in. The boss was pleased with my work.

But I sunk to some low depths. I was so lonely that I cried almost every day.

Then I met Ryan, the guy who lived in the apartments next to mine. He was cute—tall and thin, with chiseled features, very short hair, and a sexy, crooked smile. One evening I was walking the mall and we ran into each other.

"Hey, aren't you my neighbor?" he asked me.

"Yes."

"Would you like to have a beer with me?"

I paused, and then said, "Well, I don't drink beer, but I'll have a Coke."

"You don't drink beer?" he asked incredulously.

"No, but I don't drink coffee either, so at least I'm consistent."

We went to Ruby Tuesday's in the mall and ordered our drinks. We made small talk for a while. He was fun to talk to and I had a good time.

In the next few weeks, Ryan and I often ran into each other on our way in and out. Once he invited me to his apartment to watch a movie. We visited a little while, but I got nervous, so I left before we even started the movie. I got the feeling he had not expected that and might have considered me rude for leaving so early.

But he continued being friendly. He often said to me, "Hey, beautiful." Pretty soon I was crazy about him, in spite of the fact that we did not have much in common. He was handsome and quite charming, and I was very lonely.

Ryan stood me up once. I waited all evening and he never called. Then one day I saw him with another girl, holding hands. I was crushed. I cried. My chest hurt, I was so sad. The next day my dad took me to Hamby's, an old-fashioned diner downtown, for lunch. I ordered tuna, but I was so upset I could hardly eat.

I cried a lot in those days because all I ever did was go to work, then go home, then do it all again the next day.

Sunday afternoons at Mom and Dad's house used to be my happy time. My siblings and I used to meet our parents for lunch at their house, and hang out all afternoon. But then they got paired off, one by one. I was the only single left. So Sundays became a sad time for me.

8-22-99
I wish I knew how to make friends. I've been sad lately because it's lonely without a roommate.

9-3-99
I have had the most miserable week. On and off. There's been some joy, of course. But life is 90% pain and 10% joy. You have to take those good times when you can. I'm so lonely. I've cried every day this week. Today I fought tears all morning. I never have any plans. Everyone in my family who lives in Greenville has a mate except me, and I'm desperately, painfully alone. Today it seemed hopeless. When I lose my hope is when it really hurts. I wanted a way out of this life. I left the office early. When I got home I lay on my bed and cried hard. My life stretches ahead of me like a desert. Work is boring, my personal life is lonely. And the thing is I'm really trying! I'm doing my best to have a good attitude and be an attractive person, and be grateful for what I do have. And I've been calling people and trying to make plans and stay busy. But it doesn't work out. I guess I need to make even more of an effort. I knew this would happen once college ended. What's wrong with me? Can it be fixed? I feel so bad about myself. I want to believe

the day will come when I'll find someone and be happy with them, but today I've lost my hope.

9-22-99
I feel so low right now. I've been reading a book about relationships, and in so many of the bad relationships that were described, I saw myself.

10-1-99
I want to die. I just want to finish here. I am sick of this.

10-3-99
I am miserable and I cry every day. If my life doesn't change from this desolate unending loneliness, I want to die. My hope is gone, the only thing that had kept me going. I don't enjoy stuff anymore. About a month ago I was sad, but I still wanted to live. Now I don't. I keep having all these daydreams about another missing woman case. Or how I get killed in an accident with a drunk driver. Or I suddenly drop dead and it remains a mystery—nobody ever knows I died of a broken heart. I wouldn't kill myself, but I want to. At least that's what I say today, that I wouldn't do it. But I used to say I wanted to live, back when I thought it would be possible to live for real.

10-4-99
I can hardly see through the salt in my eyes. Please let tomorrow be the last sad day. I'm going to sleep, my favorite part of life.

11-11-99
I got sad because Isabel and Monica both talked excitedly about their upcoming weddings. I am happy for them and wouldn't want it any other way, but my heart is broken and it makes it so hard. I hope I never cry about it. No one should cry on their birthday.

Chapter 20: Medication

In November I told my family doctor that I'd been crying a lot, and asked if that could mean I'm depressed. He said, "Definitely," and gave me a prescription for Zoloft, an antidepressant, to take for six months.

So I had my medicine, my happy drugs. I hesitated to take the pretty little pills, because I wondered, "What happens if I swallow? Isn't pain a sign of the need to make some kind of change? If I dull the pain, will I be motivated to escape this awful, solitary lifestyle and trade it in for something better?" I know better now!

11-25-99
I'm feeling better since I started taking Zoloft. I woke up OK today.

Chapter 21: Happily Married

With the courage given to me by Zoloft, and my desire for a better, richer life, I joined a dating service so I could meet some men. I described myself as a twenty-nine-year-old, five-foot one-inch, brown-eyed and dark brown-haired Hispanic woman, with a bachelor's degree and a career as an assistant editor. I wrote that my friends would describe me as intelligent, pretty, sensitive, and kind, and that my interests were movies, books, hiking, biking, animals, shopping, travel, eating out, cooking, and home décor.

I met a few guys and went on one date with each of them. Then I got an invitation from Rob, a thirty-one-year-old, five-foot four-inch, redheaded high school teacher, who liked bicycling, reading, languages, traveling, canoeing, camping, hiking, movies, and cooking.

When I saw Rob's profile and watched his interview video, and saw how much we had in common, I thought, "I think this is my future husband!" I didn't take that thought seriously and soon forgot about it, but it came true.

Rob and I got engaged on July 2, 2001. He had cooked a Chinese meal for me in his apartment. After we ate we leaned on some pillows on the floor to watch a movie. I began to get very sleepy.

"Don't fall asleep!" panicked Rob.

"But I'm so sleepy!"

"We haven't had dessert," he said, handing me a plate of homemade fortune cookies. "I made these."

"Wow, you made them?" I said as I took one and ate it. "These are good." I read the fortune: "Love asks me no questions, and gives me endless support. Shakespeare."

"Would you like another one?"

"Just one more. I'm getting full." I took one that said, "In the end there are three things that last: faith, hope, and love. And the greatest of these is love."

Rob was eating the cookies too.

"Want one more?" he asked.

"No, thank you."

"Here, take just this one."

I took it and opened it. Inside the cookie was a diamond ring and a fortune that said, "My lover spoke and said to me, 'Arise, my darling, my beautiful one, and come with me.'"

I stared at the ring, a shocked half-smile on my face.

"Will you marry me?" Rob asked.

I dove in and said, "Yes."

On March 23, 2002, my sisters and I entered our church's brides' room, the one room in the whole church I had always wanted to use. All the girls were excitedly putting on makeup and fixing their hair, chatting and making it totally fun. Standing next to my mother looking into the mirror, I felt beautiful and loved. The photographer expertly captured everything, blending into the background of the day, doing her art. Everyone smiled and tolerated the pictures.

At noon, as I stood at the chapel entrance with my bouquet in my hands, waiting to walk down the aisle with my daddy, I began to shake. Rob's sister's boyfriend joked that there wasn't going to be anything left on the stems by the time I made it to the front.

But as soon as Lohengrin's original wedding march began, and I took my first steps down the aisle on my father's arm to meet my husband, I relaxed. The trembling stopped, and I began to enjoy the attention. Everyone stood and turned to look at me, smiling if they caught my eye. Again I felt beautiful. I saw my friends from work, my family, and colleagues of my parents. All these people had turned out to witness this miracle, as I still call it today, the miracle that I was getting married and finally getting to live.

Those first few months of married life were blissful. We completely enjoyed each other, and I loved setting up housekeeping together. I wondered why everyone said the first year of marriage would be a difficult adjustment. No, the difficult adjustment was yet to come.

Chapter 22: Benjamin

When I first began to suspect I was pregnant, I bought myself a pregnancy test and hid it in the bathroom. I didn't take it right away because I didn't want to waste it. I wanted to be sure I wasn't just late.

But after a few days I really thought I might be pregnant. All day at work I couldn't concentrate because I was too excited about going home and taking my test. When the end of the workday finally arrived, I went home and drank a lot of water so I'd have plenty of urine for the test. I took my dog Joseph for a walk while I let the water go through me.

Then, while daydreaming about something else, my nervousness temporarily forgotten, I used the toilet to relieve myself.

"Aaargh! All that trouble and now I have to start all over again and drink more water!"

Later I was ready to take my pregnancy test. I took it and waited the obligatory few minutes. Slowly the + began to appear. I looked, and looked again. It was positive. I was pregnant! I began to jump silently up and down for joy. I looked at myself in the mirror and thought, "I'm pregnant! I've never been pregnant before! I'm *pregnant*!" I was so happy. My face was flushed with joy. I had a silly smile on my face.

After a while, I was finally able to compose myself enough to come out of the bathroom. I didn't tell Rob right away because I wanted to tell him in a special way. It was hard holding onto the big wonderful secret, but I really wanted to give Rob the news over dinner. I imagined us sitting in a booth for two somewhere. I would tell him in my special way and I would get to see his reaction. I was going to make him so happy!

But Rob would not sit still. He was so frustrating. I could not pin him down. He didn't want to go out to dinner. He wanted to go to his sign language workshop. So I decided, "Fine. I'm going shopping."

I went to the Battlefield Mall. Upstairs in the children's department of Famous Barr, I bought a tiny pair of light blue Winnie the Pooh baby socks. I wanted to tell the cashier, "I just found out I'm pregnant and this is how I plan to tell my husband." But then I decided Rob should be the first to know, not some random cashier. I bought a little card with a duck on it and wrote:

To my daddy,
I wanted to buy you a present, but can I have it back when I'm born? I can't wait to meet you when I'm bigger!
I love you already,
Your baby

I gift wrapped the socks and held my precious, delicious secret until Rob finally got home. It was a cold February evening. Rob was wearing his mustard yellow coveralls.

"I have a little gift for you," I said.

"What is it?"

He kneeled on the rug in front of the fireplace. When he opened the gift and saw the little socks, then read the card, he said, "Are you pregnant?"

I said, "Yes."

"That's awesome!" he said. He hugged me and said again, "That's awesome! That's awesome!" He told me later that he almost cried.

Before becoming pregnant, I had said, "I would rather never have children than have one that turns out like me." Then at the beginning of the pregnancy, I worried and asked my youngest sister Isabel, "What if there is something wrong with this baby? I don't know if I could be proud of him."

My sister said that I would still be proud of my child, but it would just be over smaller things.

"I guess you're right," I said, and didn't think about it again.

On October 2, 2003, when the doctor announced, "three strikes and you're out, we're going to C-section," I felt relieved and afraid at the same time. I began to shake uncontrollably as events got farther out of my control and I became more vulnerable. So we careened into the operating room. Then, we heard the most wonderful, hoped-for words:

"It's a Boy!"

And so it began. Benjamin Elias Clark was gorgeous. He had reddish-brown curls all over his perfectly round head, screaming his first cries to his little world. He had big beautiful hands and feet and dark blue eyes. He was a beautiful boy. My first emotion upon meeting my son was great pride.

When we were leaving the hospital, I in my wheelchair, Benjamin in his car seat on my lap, my chest felt like it would burst. I had happy tears in my eyes. I wanted everyone to see our baby boy. Benjamin really was more than a dream come true. But those early days of being a mother were a blur of pain, exhaustion, and tears.

The biggest of my problems at this time was insomnia. As if the baby waking me weren't tiring enough, I was having trouble going back to sleep after taking care of him. Soon I began to obsess about sleep, giving wind to the flame of insomnia. I unknowingly created a monster too big to conquer alone. Here are some of my journal entries:

1-21-04
I almost fell asleep twice today, but the adrenaline zapped me back.

2-18-04
I am totally jittery and nervous and anxious and tense. It's time for bed, and I can't relax.

2-20-04
As usual, I am very tired but not sleepy. Anxiety that causes sleeplessness that causes anxiety that causes sleeplessness.

2-28-04
I had a horrible night. I did not sleep at all. I've been up for over 24 hours. I feel very tired and a little trembly, but when I try to sleep, I

feel nervous. I'm so desperate for enough consistent sleep that I'll do almost anything. I simply cannot go on like this. It's the worst! A few times during the night I blacked out for a few seconds, but then I popped right back into a nervous consciousness.

4-4-04
I woke up to go to the bathroom, and couldn't go back to sleep. About an hour later, Benjamin woke up. He was wet and hungry, so I changed his diaper and pajamas, and breastfed him. He was in a fabulous mood. I really enjoyed him. His sweetness and cuteness were a welcome break from the boredom of lying awake.

6-20-04
I was so tired all day. My body was aching but my nerves were too jangled to sleep.

I went to the doctor, complaining that I couldn't sleep. I said, "I feel like this will never end! I'll never be able to sleep again!"

He said, "I know you know this, and you wouldn't be here if you didn't, but don't do that. The more you worry about sleep, the more trouble you'll have. I'm going to give you a prescription for an antidepressant called Zoloft. Have you ever been on Zoloft before?"

"Yes," I answered. "But I'm not depressed."

"This will help you with your thoughts, and it should help you sleep." So I skeptically filled the prescription he gave me and began taking Zoloft again.

I don't know how I never realized how much I needed to be on antidepressants, not for depression, but for anxiety. I have always needed something to take the edge off and allow me to relax.

Benjamin was nine months old and becoming an easier little person to take care of. He was darling. He was a gorgeous, funny, smart baby boy. Life was definitely improving.

My parents had gone to Spain so my dad could do a sabbatical at the university of Salamanca. A wonderful opportunity came up for us to visit them for a couple of weeks. We couldn't afford the trip, but we took it anyway, and I have never regretted it. It was such a time of healing for me, and of enjoying my new little family. Benjamin, being blond and blue-eyed, attracted a lot of attention. Everyone loved him.

Salamanca held so much history. It was a beautiful town. We did a lot of sightseeing, including the place where my father was working with some of Miguel de Unamuno's writings.

We adjusted to the time change almost as soon as we arrived. I loved seeing the sun out past 10 p.m., eating supper at 11:00 and then sleeping late. Even early bird Benjamin slept until 10 every day. One of the things I remember most about the trip was how well I slept. It seems like such a silly thing now, but to me it was a big deal. Finally I felt relaxed, and normal. I felt like a normal person instead of a freak.

In the fall of 2004, my fussy baby turned into a sunny, golden little boy. He was the happiest toddler I've ever known, making everyone around him smile with his contagious laughter, enjoying his little life to the core. We loved his baby talk. "Mangmayaya" was "motorcycle," "capayaya" was "helicopter," and "fahfayaya" was butterfly.

Fall 2005 was the beginning of the "terrible twos." Benjamin's favorite phrase was "go away!" When he bumped his head, he said, "Go away, head!" When he spilled his drink at a restaurant and the server was cleaning his spill, he said, "Go away!"

He went through a kicking phase. He kicked his cousins, he kicked a man at Cici's Pizza for no apparent reason, he even kicked a little girl at Kohl's department store. Like Jerry Seinfeld said, having a 2-year-old was like having a blender without a lid. It was so much fun.

Chapter 23: Daniel

On September 11, 2005, we found out I was expecting again! We were thrilled. I loved feeling my growing child's tiny rolls, punches, and hiccups inside.

At our first ultrasound, the baby looked healthy. I was so excited when I saw it move! I saw its heart beating and its tiny feet, and its arms above its head.

The technician asked, "Do you want to know the sex?"

I said, "Oh, yes."

She paused and said, "You'd better keep all your boy clothes—it's a boy!"

"Good!" I said. I was giddy and laughing with happiness. Benjamin needed a brother. We decided to name him Daniel Joseph.

On May 12, 2006, we drove to Cox South for my C-section. It was so early it was still cool out. I was wearing my favorite black sweatshirt. Hardly anyone was there. As soon as we stepped out of the car and I saw the door to the hospital, I stopped and said, "I'm not going."

"You have to!" said Rob, "You don't have a choice now."

I knew I didn't, but still I was scared. This time I knew what lay ahead. But at 7:57 a.m., we had our new baby and I was supremely happy.

In Recovery the nurse brought me the baby to hold and try to feed him for the first time. She told me to just let him play, but when she checked on us she was surprised to find that he had latched on right away. He knew what to do! When she came back to ask if I was finished, I told her, "no." I wanted to hold him a bit longer. This was a wonderful bonding moment. I held his tiny naked body next to my skin and let him nurse. I watched his little face and stroked his soft hair. It was very sweet and I'll treasure it always.

In my hospital room I held my baby all day, watching TV, napping, and visiting with family and friends. I had that warm special glow, that new toy feeling, the rest of the day.

When Benjamin came to visit, I brightened up. "Benjamin!" I said, smiling. I couldn't wait to show him his new baby brother. I thought he would be excited. But he didn't really acknowledge the baby's presence very much. I guess it was too much to process all at once. At first Benjamin wouldn't touch me, or even approach me. Maybe the hospital bed was intimidating, or maybe he felt slightly abandoned and replaced. I don't know. But after a while he got in bed next to me and shared my spaghetti dinner. I was so pleased.

When we took Daniel home from the hospital, Benjamin rode with us. I turned around to look in the backseat at our two boys, each in his own car seat. Our family felt complete. I felt very satisfied and happy. In spite of the postpartum tears, I knew we were blessed.

Part 2

Chapter 24: A Child Like Me

For God hath not given us a spirit of fear; but of power,
and of love, and of a sound mind. 2 Timothy 1:7

It was late August 2007. It was time for Benjamin's "Meet and Greet" at Bright Minds, his new preschool. He was three years old, soon to be four. I was excited, but when we pulled into our parking space, Benjamin did not want to get out of the car. He said he didn't want to go to preschool, and he wasn't going in. It took a while, but I finally convinced him to get out of the car and go in.

As we were walking in, I pointed out the playground with the toy motorcycle, the slide, and the sandbox. Then I said, "Oh, but you don't want to use them. You don't want to come here." That got him thinking.

When we got inside, he visited the bathroom. He was impressed with the size of the toilet and sink. He said, "It's just my size!"

When we got to his classroom, though, he was very upset and cried loudly, finishing with a piercing scream. I told him, "It's OK to be nervous, but it's not OK to scream." He calmed down.

Then I showed him around. He looked at the fish and played with the toys. His teacher, talkative and friendly Mrs. Mary, showed him his basket where he could put his school supplies. He quietly put everything away and began to play. After the "Meet and Greet" we went to Culver's for ice cream and french fries, eating our treats outside at the picnic table. It was a fun morning. I had no idea of the storm we had ahead as Benjamin entered school for the first time.

It was Benjamin's first day of preschool and it was raining hard. At first he forgot what we were getting ready for as he put on his new clothes and ate his oatmeal with brown sugar.

"Where are we going?" he asked.

"To preschool," I said.

His face got serious and he said, "I don't want to go. I'm tired of it."

I said, "You've never been!" and talked to him about the toys, the fish tank, snack time, his crayons and scissors...then I left him to himself. After a while he came out of his room with his shoes on and his Star Wars backpack. He was so excited!

When we got to school, Mrs. Mary gave him a nametag and showed him where to hang his backpack, and then I left!

Later, when I picked him up, his teacher walked him to the car and told me he had done great. She said, "He was quiet and cooperative, and that's what we like to see." When she asked him if he was ready to come back to school next time, he nodded his head.

As soon as we drove off, Benjamin began telling me all about school. The conversation continued at lunch at his favorite chicken restaurant, Chick-fil-A. He said he cut Holiday Bear out with his scissors. He played with the pretend food, but then he didn't want to play with the food, so they went to the playroom, where he didn't want to ride the train. They had honey sticks and juice for a snack.

A few days into the school year, when Mrs. Mary brought Benjamin to my car, she said, "You know, I don't think I've ever heard his voice. He doesn't talk to me."

"Does he talk to the other kids?" I asked.

"No," she said, shaking her head, almost apologetically. She seemed mystified and a little concerned.

"I didn't talk in school until the third grade," I said.

"So the apple didn't fall far from the tree," said Mrs. Mary.

I made light of the situation, but I was very sad.

Not only did Benjamin not talk in school, he had trouble in other situations, too. One time he was invited to a birthday party at Gymboree. There were fun slides, balance beams, trampolines, foam blocks— everything a preschool child would love. Benjamin loved those things! But he would not join in. When we tried to get him to play the party games, he got very upset. He just sat there when it was his turn, looking terrified and shaking his head "no," with tears brimming in his eyes. He could not enjoy that party, or any other birthday party he was invited to.

One night as I was tucking Benjamin into his bed for the night, he told me that one of the kids at church had spit on him.

"Did you tell him to stop?" I asked.

"No, I was too shy," he said.

My chest hurt right then. How sad it was that he could not defend himself from getting spit on! I knew what that was like, but it hurt even more when it was my child.

I felt so bad for Benjamin because I knew from experience his agony. It's such a prison, and it leads to wasted potential. I wanted life's opportunities to be available to him, not out of his reach because he never learned to manage his fear.

I felt like we were in a hopeless crisis with this. It hurt to think that all my bad memories could become Benjamin's bad experiences. I did not want him to experience the shame, the fear, the sadness, the frustration, or the loneliness. I had hoped my children would escape that. But I was learning that children are very much like their parents, in the good and in the bad.

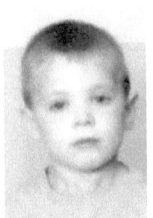

Chapter 25: The Revelation

It was winter, sometime after Christmas 2007. Our relatives from Rob's side of the family were sitting around the living room, relaxing and visiting.

"How is Benjamin doing in school?" Rob's brother's fiancé, Angela, asked me.

"He's doing fine," I answered, smiling.

"Does he talk in school?"

"No," I said, feeling sad. "He's too much like me."

Then Angela told me about a segment she had seen on television about children who talk perfectly well at home, but are mute in school and outside the home where they're not comfortable. I was immediately interested. My mother-in-law had seen the segment too. It took them a while to remember what it was called, but when they remembered and told me, I did some Internet research, and found a website that explained everything: www.selectivemutism.org.

Selective Mutism Group ~ Childhood Anxiety Network

Do you know a child who can talk freely at home but appears frozen in other settings like at school or out in public?

Do you know a child who seems so shy that they take a very long time to warm up in social situations, if at all? Does it seem out of the normal range of shyness you observe in other children? If so, you may know a child with Selective Mutism and you've come to the right place.

Whether you are a parent of a child with SM, a teacher of a SM student, a therapist with a SM patient or anyone interested in learning more, SMG can help. We are the nation's premier resource for SM information, providing a network of families and treating professionals across the world who uniquely understand the struggles of SM. Stop struggling alone. Start seeking information and new ideas. Help us Rid the Silence!

Through this website I learned that Selective Mutism is a childhood social communication anxiety disorder. It is much more than shyness; it is social phobia. Selective Mutism is NOT a child willfully refusing to talk. I had just found answers to so many questions, and best of all those answers gave us hope! Our child, just like myself as a child and young adult, was more than just shy. It went deeper and darker than that. He had Social Anxiety Disorder.

My eyes did not blink and my mind did not stray as I stared at the computer. I thought about the pain of being "beyond shy" all my life, the memories crashing into each other, along with a grand feeling of epiphany. I felt overwhelmed and hopeful at the same time. Chemicals hurt my veins, my arms, and my insides, keeping me awake and reeling all night.

I barely slept that night because of all the thoughts flying around in my head.

Chapter 26: Therapy, The Next Generation

After our revelation, we began a long process of helping our son. The first thing we did was to order some books from the Selective Mutism Group's bookstore. I gave Benjamin's teacher, Mrs. Mary, the book *The Ideal Classroom Setting for the Selectively Mute Child*.

Mrs. Mary went above her call of duty to help us, using the information from the book I gave her. She allowed us to stay after school with Benjamin to hang out in the classroom and play. I hoped it would help him feel more comfortable at school, and get used to hearing his own voice there. He talked, but only to his brother or me, and only when he thought nobody could hear him.

On our second or third visit, Mrs. Mary stayed within earshot, so she could hear Benjamin talk. Benjamin, Daniel, and I were on the floor playing with some trucks and robots.

"This robot's gonna drive the truck, and he has guns on his arms," said Benjamin. He drove the truck around the floor, making sound effects, forgetting, or maybe not realizing, that his teacher was nearby.

Pretty soon Benjamin and Daniel started fighting over a toy. They both grabbed it and were pulling on it.

"Who had it first?" I asked.

"I did," said Benjamin.

"Noo! Me!" said Daniel.

Mrs. Mary chuckled and said, "Of course they both say that."

Benjamin said with mild indignation, "I don't want her to laugh at me."

I said, "Nobody's laughing at you, Benjamin."

Mrs. Mary said, "I'm not laughing at you."

During another of Benjamin's after school visits, Mrs. Mary said, "That was fun for me! I've never heard his voice before! He's a normal four-year-old boy!"

"He is," I said, smiling happily. "He just needs to be in the right situation."

I was learning so much from the educational materials I had found about Selective Mutism. After doing some reading on the subject, I felt bad that I had actually said to Benjamin, "It's rude to not answer people when they talk to you!" I did not realize how much pressure that must have put on him, until I learned that trying to make him speak only increased his anxiety.

I did not hesitate to spend money when it came to helping Benjamin. I bought him a "clip talker," so he could record himself saying something, then play it back to someone. He used it at school for show and tell once. He loved that thing.

I learned that play dates are the most important thing you can do to help your child begin to talk at school. The idea is that you invite one child to come to your home, and after a few play dates, your selectively mute child will be able to talk to that one child.

Then you have a play date at school, until your child can talk to that child at school.

Then you invite another child to your home, and then have a play date at school, until your child with SM can talk to two children at school.

You keep adding children to the little group until your child can talk at school. In other words, gradually desensitize your child to social interaction.

Asking for a play date was one of my biggest fears, especially when I don't know the people! But this is what I had to do, and it is amazing what one will do for the love of one's child. I knew I could no longer fear initiating social interaction. My fear and my pride had to die, like the beautiful leaves of fall, so that Benjamin could thrive.

So I arranged a play date with a boy in Benjamin's preschool class named David. Benjamin often told me how much he liked David, that David was his friend, and that he played with David. David's mother told me she had asked her son if Benjamin ever talked to him, and David replied, "No, but I talk to him."

When the day of the play date came, I was so nervous that I could hardly eat. My hands were cold. I kept having to go to the bathroom. It was ridiculous, really. I couldn't believe something so small could make me so afraid. And it didn't help that they were very late. I kept looking out the window and trying to play with Benjamin and Daniel, but I just could not focus very well. Finally, they showed up.

I showed them in and called Benjamin into the living room. It was awkward at first, because Benjamin would not talk to David, but David talked and played with Benjamin anyway. We got them started with some toys, and it wasn't long before they were having a good time.

David was still doing most of the talking, but every once in a while, toward the end of the play date, I heard Benjamin's voice. It was like a miracle happening in my home. I grinned. It was a beginning. I felt a little taller, lighter, and warmer.

For the school year 2008-2009, Benjamin was in a Pre-K class at Bright Minds in the yellow room with Mrs. Kristy. I had met Audrey at the Meet and Greet, whose son Jonathan was one of Mrs. Kristy's suggestions for a possible friend for Benjamin. So I called her and arranged a play date.

It went pretty well! At first Benjamin did not talk to Jonathan. We all sat awkwardly in the living room for a few minutes, showing Jonathan some of Benjamin's toys to break the ice. But after a while, they began playing together. I thought I even heard Benjamin's voice from his bedroom! And Audrey turned out to be very friendly and easy to talk to.

Audrey made it easy to continue the play dates. Sometimes she invited us over, and sometimes I invited them to our place. My boys loved going over to Jonathan's house to play. Other kids' toys always seem more exciting than one's own.

Benjamin eventually talked to Jonathan, even at Jonathan's house, as if there had never been a problem. He talked and laughed, ran and played, like a normal kid, as long as nobody else was around.

At school, Mrs. Kristy began pairing Benjamin up with Jonathan whenever she could. During Show and Tell in April, the teacher had Benjamin whisper to Jonathan what he wanted to say to the class, and Jonathan told everyone what Benjamin had whispered. It worked so well that we both wished we had more time in the school year. We wondered why we had not tried it earlier.

All the while, I kept studying our materials on Selective Mutism (SM) and Social Anxiety Disorder. In addition to educating ourselves, we had to educate the string of therapists we took Benjamin to. Nobody in our area had any experience treating children with SM, and many had not even heard of it.

The first therapist we tried told us he only worked with adults (the receptionist who gave us the appointment dropped the ball on that one).

The second therapist normally worked with children with behavioral disorders, and she treated Benjamin as if his silence were misbehavior.

The third therapist used play therapy to get Benjamin more comfortable with her, but did nothing to help him overcome his fears outside of her office. The fourth was the same.

Our most helpful resources were the books and videos that helped us come up with a plan to desensitize Benjamin to the social situations he feared. They included progress charts to fill in as we carried out his therapy (from the SMART Center—Selective Mutism Anxiety Research and Treatment Center).

We used this progress chart (adapted a little) when we went to a restaurant. In addition to giving Benjamin the practice he needed, it gave us a good excuse to eat out!

Restaurant	Nod, Point, Gesture, Show	Tell parent my order close up	Tell parent my order fist length away	Tell parent my order ½ arm length away	Tell parent my order full arm length away	I gave my order!
Old Chicago, 4/10/09	X (food)					X (drink)
Little Tokyo, 5/10/09						X (drink)
Arris' Pizza, 5/27/09					X	
Pizza Hut, 6/15/09						X (drink)

We always made Benjamin place his own order. If he couldn't verbalize to the server what he wanted, he would point to the item on the menu, or draw a picture of what he wanted. And if he wanted a Coke, he had to order it himself, verbally. Sometimes he ended up drinking water, and other times he wanted the Coke badly enough to ask for it.

So he was making progress, but his progress was slow and limited. We still met with resistance often, especially if he was in a bad mood. We were slogging along, hoping and praying for a miracle—that Benjamin's wings would take him farther than my broken ones ever took me.

When Benjamin had a success, I was so proud of him! It hit me then that no matter what, I was proud of this boy. I loved him fiercely. I wanted the world to know he was mine, imperfections and all. But I still desperately wanted him to overcome this fear, and several things got in the way of his progress.

First, it is nearly impossible to teach your children skills you yourself do not possess. Remember my issues as a schoolchild? And as a young adult trying to become a professional, and wishing for a family of my own? I had lived with an unaddressed anxiety disorder for over thirty years. What kind of an example could I be?

Second, I was learning that we do have brain chemistry imbalances running in our family, on both sides. For generations, many of my family members have suffered from anxiety or depression. My paternal grandmother was told that if she would "get right with God," she would not be depressed. I think it's sad that she believed that, and felt unworthy of taking communion at her church like she wanted. Too many of us had been misunderstood, and I was just happy that it stopped here, with our firstborn son.

I wanted to try medication with Benjamin, but I wanted it to be a last resort. Medication is not without risks, and the long-term effects are not known. But we do know the long-term effects of not treating a social anxiety disorder: isolation, depression, drug and alcohol abuse, and in the worst cases, suicide. I was actually blessed in the way my life turned out. But I wanted even better for my son.

So in late May I brought up the issue of medication with the Ask the Doc therapist online. I described how we had been working with Benjamin for a year and a half to help him overcome his SM. I described his improvements and his trouble spots. I wanted to know how we could encourage him to try the next hardest thing, and what we could do when he refused to try. I told the therapist that we always reminded Benjamin of the rewards he could earn if he tried, but sometimes that was not enough of a motivator. I asked, "Do you have any suggestions? Is it normal for progress to move this slowly?"

In early June we got our e-mail response from the therapist. She said that a year and a half is a very long time for progress to still be moving slowly, and that something had to shift. We could not go on forever stuck at that stage. So she suggested the use of "bravery bucks." These look like play money but are given for any brave act, not just talking. This helps take the focus off the talking, so the child does not feel pressured. So we set up a prize system where every so many bravery bucks earned Benjamin a prize he really wanted.

Then the therapist online told us that we needed to consider adding medication to the treatment plan. She reminded us that medication takes the edge off the child's anxiety and increases their success with treatment. Once momentum is achieved, the child can be taken off the medication and the momentum usually continues.

When I brought up the issue of medication with Benjamin's therapist, he thought it was a good idea too. He said he wanted to suggest it, but he wanted it to be our idea. He then referred us to a child psychiatrist.

Chapter 27: Success!

In June of 2009, we put Benjamin on a low dose of generic Prozac. What a difference! Almost overnight, Benjamin was a different child, the child he was at home, only without the rage of his tantrums.

In early July, Benjamin was invited to his neighbor's birthday party. In the past at Aiden's parties, Benjamin has stuck close to me, never talking or playing with the other kids. Birthday parties were painful for him and for me, because I knew what he was going through. I could tell he wanted so badly to join in, but he just couldn't.

This time, he got in the wading pool with the other kids. Instead of his blank or sometimes angry expression, his face was smiling. He talked and splashed and played with his friends. I sat there smiling and watching the miracle blossom, hardly able to believe what I was seeing.

The best part was how happy he was. He couldn't stop talking about his "medicine that helps me relax and talk."

After the birthday boy opened his presents, his mother said to him, "Aiden, tell everybody 'thank you' for the gifts." Aiden looked uncomfortable for a moment, and he looked down.

Benjamin joyfully said, "Aiden, maybe you could try the medicine I take. It helps me not be scared so I can talk."

I was slightly embarrassed about this; Benjamin didn't know that people aren't interested in your medications, or that Aiden did not have severe social phobia as he did. All Benjamin knew was that finally he could partake in the joys life has to offer. No longer would he be frustrated, alone, and unable to speak his mind or join in the fun. He just couldn't keep it inside. He wanted to tell everyone.

My friend Julie, the birthday boy's mother, said, "Susanna, you must be so happy! I bet you want to cry." When she said that, I did feel tears of joyful emotion. Julie's misgivings about putting a child on psychiatric medication melted right then. She was a believer too.

Normally in the past, when we went to the park, Benjamin avoided groups of children, preferring a less crowded part of the park. As soon as someone approached us, Benjamin got serious and quiet, and wanted to leave. This changed after he started medication.

One day at the park near our house, there were a bunch of boys playing ball. Excited about his new social skills, Benjamin approached the boys and asked if he could play. They tossed him the ball, and before I knew it, he was running and playing with the other kids. I stood amazed and watched my little boy live life.

Then at the jungle gym, he met another boy. He started a conversation: "Hi. Do you have a video game system? We do." His first flights were a little awkward, but it wasn't long before he blended in perfectly. He loved it, and so did I.

Benjamin also began talking at church. One Sunday after class, his teacher said to me, "I've never seen Benjamin so talkative. He did great!"

He talked at Vacation Bible School at our neighbor friends' church. The teacher (his friend's mother) said, "It was like there was never an issue. He did great."

Benjamin placed his own orders at restaurants. He confidently told the pharmacist that he wanted watermelon flavor for his medicine. He talked at Kindermusik, in front of the whole group, something that was unheard of before medication. He initiated greetings with people he had just met.

To someone else, all this was everyday stuff. But not to us—these were all miracles to us! And still today I don't take it for granted.

We had decided to put Benjamin in the Kindergarten program at Bright Minds, where he had gone to preschool, even though it was expensive for us. We thought he needed a smaller class situation. I had been saving money for a long time, tiny bit by tiny bit. And just in time, we saved enough money to pay the Kindergarten tuition.

Benjamin's Kindergarten year holds a special magic for me because it was such a turning point. On Meet and Greet day, I wondered how Benjamin would react to a new class situation. I was prepared to have to start all over again with his therapy, introducing him to one child at a time until he felt comfortable enough to eventually use his voice at school. I kept imagining the possibilities as we walked up the stairs and around the hallway to his new classroom. Even though he had shocked us all with his newfound voice in the summer, I did not expect he had bloomed enough to continue that in a new setting. I wondered if he would feel overwhelmed.

But when we opened the door and walked into his new Kindergarten room, the first thing that happened was that a very outgoing child came over to us and said, "Hi, I'm Colton. How old are you?" The moment after that question felt longer to me than it surely was, almost as if there should have been a drumroll.

Then Benjamin answered, "Five."

"He's talking!" I celebrated in my mind. I was so relieved and happy.

Benjamin had not wanted to go to his Meet and Greet. He had been nervous, afraid he wasn't going to like Kindergarten, and he had responded with his usual defiance. But when we got there and toured the classroom, looking at the different learning centers and school supplies, he got excited. "You were right, Mommy. This is fun!" he said. That was a happy moment for me.

We met the teacher, Mrs. Victoria, a popular teacher with years of experience, and I gave her some information on Selective Mutism and told her our past troubles. "You may not even need this information," I told her, "but here it is just in case." It turned out that I was right—it would have been fine for her not to know about Benjamin's history, because Benjamin did perfectly fine.

I will never forget Mrs. Victoria's words after a few weeks of school: "If you hadn't told me there had been a problem, I would never have guessed."

Chapter 28: Helping Daniel

Just as Benjamin's friend Jonathan was instrumental in Benjamin's success (they are still good friends), Benjamin helped his little brother Daniel overcome his social fears.

When Daniel started preschool, he cried a lot the first few days. A helper had to hold him on her lap until he calmed down. Then one day he stopped crying. But what he turned to then wasn't much better. It was just quieter.

The evening of the parent meeting and open house, Daniel's teacher, Mrs. Dana, said that Daniel wasn't talking or playing with the other kids. He stuck close to her the whole time. She told me, "He's alone."

My chest felt crushed at her words. I was so very sad that I wanted to cry. We had been down this road before, and it was so hard. I didn't want my son to be "alone." I was relieved right then that we weren't going to have any more children, because our struggles were great and I couldn't imagine going through it all again.

So to help Daniel, I worked up the nerve again to invite one of the mothers and her son Isaiah, Daniel's classmate, over to our house for a play date. It was fun. We all had a lot in common. Isaiah even had an older brother who was in Benjamin's Kindergarten class. Kindergarten started their day a half hour earlier than preschool, so Daniel had a built-in play date with his new buddy every preschool morning. It was made easy for us that way, so working on Daniel's therapy was not nearly as much of a struggle as Benjamin's. Plus we already knew how to handle a "child who doesn't talk."

We noticed that when Benjamin got on medication and overcame his Selective Mutism, Daniel started to do better too! Other people noticed it as well. By the end of Daniel's second year of preschool, his teacher said, "Boy, things have changed! Daniel is Mr. Popular now. Everyone wants to sit by him!" What a feeling!

Chapter 29: Redemption

There is a good side to Benjamin's and my personalities! Elaine Aron's book *The Highly Sensitive Person* brought me validation and self-esteem. In her book, she describes a highly sensitive person as someone who has a sensitive nervous system, can sense subtle changes in his or her surroundings, and is easily overwhelmed by a stimulating environment. The trait is not a defect, but an asset.

Some characteristic behaviors are:

- Being easily overwhelmed by bright lights, strong odors, coarse fabrics, or loud noises
- Getting flustered when there is a lot to do and not enough time
- Avoiding violent movies and TV shows
- Needing to withdraw during busy days for privacy and relief
- Avoiding upsetting situations
- Noticing and enjoying delicate flavors, aromas, sounds, or works of art
- Having a rich and complex inner life
- Being seen as sensitive or shy

This describes Benjamin and me perfectly! I realize now that I was just a highly sensitive child who was overwhelmed by her world, and so was my son.

Finally, I can look at Benjamin's and my natural temperament in a positive way. I have learned the good side of being so sensitive. Benjamin is very compassionate. He cannot watch suffering and just ignore it. If someone looks cold, he will bring that person a blanket. If he notices a cut on someone's finger, he will bring that one a bandage. When Daniel had pinkeye, Benjamin brought him a wet washcloth, let him choose whether to go first or second at bath time, drew him a picture, and brought him a toy. When our dog Joseph died of cancer, I was with him while he died. When I was sure he was gone, I broke down and cried. Three-year-old Benjamin asked me, "Mommy, why are you crying?"

"Because Joseph died," I said.

Benjamin said to me, "I'll fly my kite for you to make you feel better." And he did. Benjamin has a very big heart. And now that he is learning how to conquer his weaknesses, the strengths of his personality can come out. His traits are being used for good instead of holding him back.

Through Benjamin's overcoming he did a beautiful thing for me. Because I was not my culture's ideal, I grew up not liking myself. I was ashamed of the way I had been. But because Benjamin started showing the same problems I had, we were finally able to figure out what had been plaguing our family for generations—anxiety and depression disorders. Now because of what we know, I can accept myself, I can appreciate the good side of being so sensitive, and I can find help.

Our pastor once said that if we suffer, someone down the line will not. And if we do not suffer, someone before us did. My life story, and that of our son, explains just how true our pastor's statement was.

I believe God used the pain of my youth for something good: I was highly motivated to do whatever it took to help my child. And he, just by existing, has helped not only me but other family members as well. The pain of my childhood has been redeemed.

Read More

Aron, Elaine. *The Highly Sensitive Person: How to Thrive When the World Overwhelms You.* New York: Carol Pub., 1996.

McHolm, Angela E., Charles E. Cunningham, and Melanie K. Vanier. *Helping Your Child With Selective Mutism: Practical Steps to Overcome a Fear of Speaking.* Oakland, CA: New Harbinger Publications, 2005.

Shipon-Blum, Elisa. *The Ideal Classroom Setting for the Selectively Mute Child.* Philadelphia, PA: Selective Mutism Anxiety Research and Treatment Center.

Shipon-Blum, Elisa. *Selective Mutism and Social Anxiety Disorder: Learning to Socialize and Communicate within the Real World.* Two Audio CDs and CD-ROM with pdf handout.

Shipon-Blum, Elisa. *The Selective Mutism Conference: Understanding and Treating Selective Mutism and Development of School-Based Accommodations/ Interventions (IEPs & 504 Plans).* Four Disc Presentation.

Useful Web Sites
 http://www.socialanxietysupport.com/
 http://www.worrywisekids.org/
 http://www.childanxiety.net/
 http://www.adaa.org/
 http://www.selectivemutism.org/

www.ingramcontent.com/pod-product-compliance
Lightning Source LLC
Chambersburg PA
CBHW021545290526
45785CB00004BA/1525